Trust and Obey

Peter H. Noble

New Wine Press

New Wine Press
PO Box 17
Chichester
West Sussex PO20 6YB
England

All Scripture quotations are taken from the Revised Standard Version, © copyright 1952 and 1971.

ISBN: 1 874367 42 6

Typeset by CRB Associates, Norwich
Printed in England by Clays Ltd, St Ives plc

For ever, O Lord, Thy word is firmly fixed in the heavens.
(Psalm 119:89)

Scripture cannot be broken.
(John 10:35)

Dedication

This book is written to the glory of God
through Jesus Christ our Lord
and dedicated to my wife, Margaret,
without whose prayers and encouragement
it would never have been started or completed.

Contents

	Foreword	6
	Preface	7
Chapter 1	The God Who Heals	9
Chapter 2	Learning Along the Way	18
Chapter 3	Blagley	25
Chapter 4	New Lives	31
Chapter 5	The Power to Live	35
Chapter 6	In All Things by Prayer	42
Chapter 7	Signs and Wonders	53
Chapter 8	Commitment	61
Chapter 9	Simple Obedience in Small Things	66
Chapter 10	Mammon	72
Chapter 11	Ministry	79
Chapter 12	And the Greatest of These	85
	Epilogue	94

Foreword

There are many books written about mega-churches, offering mega-answers that do not have a great deal to say to the average Christian attempting to bear his or her witness in ordinary situations.

What Peter Noble has to tell us is in marked contrast. He is not writing about a superchurch. He is writing about his ministry and the ministry of a church in a mining vlllage, which, in the hands of the Holy Spirit, demonstrated what God was able to do when His people let Him have the opportunity. For this reason the book will be a challenge and an encouragement to anyone who reads it.

Over a period of ten years I had the privilege of visiting his parish on many occasions and getting to know members of the church well. I can only say that Peter is writing about spiritual realities. I have rarely visited a church in which loving relationships were so tangible. It was a church in which many came to faith in Christ, and a church which showed tremendous care for the community. It was a church which had an authentic New Testament atmosphere.

So read this account of a twenty year ministry. You cannot fail to read it with profit.

Bill Persson
Bishop of Doncaster 1982–92

Preface

'Everyone then who hears these words of mine and does them will be like a wise man who built his house upon the rock.' (Matthew 7:24)

This book has one aim – to show the Bible is true.

Scripture has a truth which cannot be shown by intellectual theological argument, but rather in lives of trusting obedience.

If we take the Bible at face value, and seek to obey it, then God is found to be as good as His Word.

This was our experience as we ministered for twenty years, from 1972, in a South Yorkshire mining parish, which we call Blagley. The illustrations used are true stories from that time of ministry. Some names, including the name of the parish, have been changed.

All Scripture points to Jesus, and it is my prayer and hope that this book may, in some small way, lead the reader closer to Him.

Peter Noble

Chapter 1

The God Who Heals

'I am the Lord, your healer.'   (Exodus 15:26)

'Are you the Vicar, then?', said a Yorkshire voice behind me.

I was in a local café one mid-week morning. We had been in Blagley for about two years, and I was getting used to the idea that I really was the Vicar. As I turned round, there stood a middle-aged man, waving his hand at me.

'Look at this hand,' he said.

I looked. It was covered with sores.

'Will you pray for it?'

'Of course,' said I, vaguely thinking that I would say a prayer when I got back home, or perhaps pop into the church and pray there.

But a little voice inside said, 'Pray for it now.'

'I can't do that,' I thought. The café was full of people. What would they think if some crazy Vicar suddenly started to pray!

Yet the voice kept on at me, 'Pray for it now.'

So I made a bargain.

'OK Lord, I will pray for it now, provided everybody leaves the café.'

To my amazement, as soon as I made this bargain, all the

9

customers got up and left! I was astounded, and not a little fearful.

My new friend, Gordon, also made to go.

'Well, I'll be off,' he said.

So with my heart in my boots, I said 'Hang on, I'll just say a prayer for your hand now.'

I do not know who was the most surprised, Gordon, myself, or the lady behind the counter. However, I took hold of his hand, and said a prayer asking for the Lord's healing. Whether I believed the Lord would heal is known only to Him.

Gordon then went, and I made a quick getaway back to the safety of the Vicarage.

The following Sunday evening, I was standing outside the church before Evensong. A group of people were coming up the church path. As they went into church a man at the back of the group stopped. It was Gordon.

'Look at this hand,' he said. 'Gone.'

No, not the hand, but the sores. They had completely gone. His hand had been healed. It happened soon after I prayed for him.

I had believed for many years that the Lord could and would heal through prayer. He says, 'I am the Lord your healer.' I believed that the healing miracles of Jesus were true, and that in the power of His Spirit, people could be used to bring His healing today. I had even known a priest in Huddersfield who had a powerful healing ministry.

But I never thought the Lord could use me. I had imagined it was only the really holy men whom the Lord used in this way; people who spent hours in prayer and who glowed with His presence. He would certainly not use an inadequate, new clergyman like me. I also thought that people used in healing would have to work themselves up into a suitably high spiritual state before they could lay on hands. It could not happen through a prayer said rather hastily in a café.

Yet the evidence was there. It had happened. Gordon's hand was better. The truth of the promise of Jesus, recorded in Mark 16:18 that *'They will lay their hands on the sick, and they will recover'* had been shown to me.

That was not the end of this particular incident. Next Sunday morning Gordon arrived at church again. He was hobbling as he walked up the path.

'You'll have to pray for my feet now,' he said. 'It's broken out there as well.'

This really was a potentially faith-shattering experience. I let Gordon go into the church and wondered whatever to do next.

At the end of the service, I took the Vicar's usual place in the church porch. When Gordon came out, I grabbed him, and taking another church member with me, whisked him round the corner. Hoping no one would see us, we laid hands on Gordon and prayed that as the Lord had healed his hand, would He please also heal his feet.

The following Sunday, Gordon arrived with healed feet. All was well. A sigh of relief emanated from a Vicar who was getting into deep water. After that Gordon came regularly to church, morning and evening, until the time of his death, about eighteen years later.

This was my first experience of the power of the Lord to heal, and it led to many other things. Above all it gave me a new confidence, although I had no idea what to do next.

A great help towards understanding the healing ministry came at a Parish Weekend led by Cecil Cousen from the Fountain Trust. Cecil taught about healing, and laid on hands for emotional as well as physical healing. We ended the weekend with a wonderful healing service, the first I had ever experienced.

All this was a deep learning experience. My eyes were

opened to the power of the spiritual gifts of the word of knowledge and the word of wisdom. Whilst laying on hands for emotional healing, Cecil said various words to each person kneeling at the altar rail. These people were all church members, whom he did not know, yet his words were exactly right for each one of them. It was as if Cecil had known them all their lives, and had intimate knowledge of their problems.

I saw from that moment that the gifts of the Spirit were tools of the trade; weapons with which to fight the battles of the Lord. They were not for show, or public exhibition, but for loving and quiet use to bring God's people to that wholeness of body, mind and spirit for which our Lord longs.

I also learned of the power of the Lord to heal at a distance. Our nephew, Peter, was seven months old, and seriously ill in hospital. He could not take food, and was dehydrating at an alarming rate. The doctors were unable to find the cause or the cure for the problem. My wife, Margaret, received the laying on of hands for Peter at the healing service. He began to improve the very next day, and was completely healed after several weeks. This amazed the doctors, who had said he might grow out of it by the time he was seven, but could not give any guarantees. No medical reason was found for his cure.

This was our first experience of 'distance healing', although the Centurion with a sick servant, and the Syro-Phoenician woman with her demon-possessed daughter, knew all about it. We realised what is self-evident in the Scriptures, that the Lord is not limited by distance. He has only to say the word, and our loved ones will be healed, wherever they are.

After Cecil's visit, we marched into the healing ministry with increased knowledge and great enthusiasm. As well as praying for the sick by name during normal Sunday intercessions, we dared to hold the occasional healing service. Hands were laid on sick people as the need arose, and members of the church were encouraged to pray for the sick. We still had much to learn, but the Lord was patient and gentle with us.

We discovered in James, chapter 5, clear and simple instructions for anointing the sick with oil.

> *'Is any among you sick? Let him call for the elders of the church, and let them pray over him, anointing him with oil in the name of the Lord; and the prayer of faith will save the sick man, and the Lord will raise him up.'*
>
> (James 5:14, 15)

We saw anointing with oil as a matter of simple obedience to the Word of God. This is what God said, therefore this is what we had to do, trusting Him to carry out His promise.

There were many surprises along the way as we sought to obey God. The first time I preached about anointing I was cornered by the Lord. It was at Evensong. After my sermon we had the normal offertory hymn, and after receiving the plate, I turned to give the blessing. There, kneeling at the altar rail was Paula. She was a young lady who had just started coming to church, and was ill with a nervous disorder.

I looked at her, wondering what was going on. A member of the church who was standing by her said,

'Paula wants to be anointed now.'

I had not expected such an immediate response to my sermon, and I had no idea what to do. Thankfully there was a bottle of olive oil in the church, so I announced to the congregation that we would now anoint Paula, and would they please kneel for prayer. I anointed her, saying an extempore prayer and applying the oil with a trembling hand. I hoped I had done it right. Paula was healed, although it did not happen instantly.

Here is the acid test. Are people healed? There is little point in proclaiming a ministry of healing, if people are not healed. The answer, in our experience was, yes, very many, by the power and grace of God.

Healing came in a variety of ways. Sometimes the results were more or less instantaneous.

Elsie was a cousin who lived in Huddersfield. She was suffering from rheumatoid arthritis as a result of a road accident, and was so ill that every morning she had to be put into a bath of warm water before she could move. We were prompted to write to her, and as a result Elsie came to be anointed one Sunday evening. There was no apparent improvement at the anointing, but afterwards at the Vicarage, we all heard Elsie's bones grating. Travelling back to Huddersfield in the car, Elsie's hands and feet started to tingle with renewed circulation, and she began to feel warm. On arriving home, just two hours after the service, she could touch her toes. She got up at half past six the following morning, with no pain, stiffness or tiredness. She was healed. The rheumatoid arthritis had gone and it never returned.

Three weeks later there was an unexpected bonus. Elsie had been born with a twisted spastic foot. Suddenly it went back into place. Her foot, like the rest of her body was healed. There was great rejoicing, and every year, at the anniversary of her healing, Elsie would return to Blagley with a thanksgiving offering. She said,

'Brian says he has a happier wife, and our boys say they have a new mum. We praise and thank the Lord for this blessing He has given us.'

Andrew was a young child of a church member. He was covered with warts, so much so that he was a figure of fun at school. His mother brought him to church one Sunday morning, asking that we please anoint him, to get rid of his warts.

We anointed him, and by next Sunday the warts had disappeared. Not one was left. His sunburned skin was now covered with little white marks, where the warts had been; although a few days of sunshine sorted that out. To dispel any future doubt, his mother, in great faith, had taken a photograph of Andrew before his anointing. She then took another one, a week later, just to record a miracle from our God.

Sometimes healing came slowly, over a period of weeks or even months.

Doreen suffered from depression. She was suicidal and cried a lot. Every time she came to church she sobbed and sobbed. We anointed her, prayed for her and talked with her. Various church members encouraged her, comforted her, and sought to counsel her. But still she was depressed. Yet she faithfully came to church, and also to a mid-week prayer group. She would sob all the way through that too.

Then, suddenly, one day at the prayer group she prayed, 'Lord, I thank you that you have given me two good days.'

That was it. Doreen was healed. Her two good days became a week, a month, and a year. All the tears went. She became bright and open. Her prayers were full of joy. She laughed, and caused us to laugh. Instead of being ministered to, she started to care for others in need. It was a complete transformation.

We cannot always understand the ways of the Lord, but it was now clear, even to us, that He had been working in Doreen all this time. We could not see what was happening, but overnight He showed us a beautiful new person, leaving us gasping with amazement and joy.

On many occasions the healing was internal and could not be seen. Over the years we anointed about twenty women who were worried about lumps in their breasts. Each was anointed just before they were due to see a specialist. On every occasion one of two results occurred. Either the lump completely disappeared, or remained but was benign. In no case was a cancer diagnosed. Some would call this coincidence, but we knew that it was the Lord acting through the simple obedience of His people to His Word.

There were times when the Lord brought healing in ways which were completely beyond anything we could conceive.

Annie, a well loved member of the church, was due to have a major heart operation. We prayed for her before she went into hospital, and felt sure she would be fine.

The operation took place on a Thursday, and when we met together in church on the Sunday, she had still not come round from the anaesthetic. The atmosphere in the church was one of deep gloom. What had gone wrong? Was she going to die? I must have been given a gift of faith that day, for with great confidence I said we must trust God, and not be despondent. We prayed again for Annie, and asked for her healing.

When it was time to receive Communion, one of our church members, Ivy, was given a shock. She was at the head of the queue, waiting to kneel at the altar rail. As she looked at those kneeling and receiving the Sacrament she saw Annie! After a few seconds confusion, she looked again. Of course it was not Annie, how could it be? It was Betty, one of our newer members. Ivy mentioned this strange experience to Betty after the service. Betty looked amazed and confused.

'How odd,' she said. 'As I knelt at the rail I asked the Lord if I could take Communion for Annie this morning.'

Annie came round that very hour.

We cannot say what was going on in the spiritual realm at that time, but we do know the Lord was working through His church, and especially through Betty, to bring healing to Annie.

Frank was a retired miner, dying in hospital from melanoma. He was not a church member, but one of his sons, another Frank, was a new and enthusiastic Christian. One Sunday evening, the younger Frank was anointed in church for his father.

That night, father Frank suffered a lot. He was covered with sweat and was very uncomfortable. But when the nurses tried to change his clothes they felt sensations like electric shocks coming from his body. It was as if he were alive with power. Even the bed on which he was lying gave the nurses shocks; so much so that they called for a maintenance man, to see if there were any electrical connections touching the bed. There were none.

The next morning the nurses mentioned this phenomenon to a doctor. He asked them,

'Does he go to church?'

The doctor told them that he had come across this experience once before, where the patient was a committed church member.

Within a few days Frank was sent home. As things turned out, the disease was in remission, but Frank lived a further six years or more. Like King Hezekiah of old, the Lord had added years to his life. Those years were well used, for Frank came to a saving faith in Jesus, and when he died, it was as a Christian man who was safe in the arms of his Lord.

Through the ministry of healing we were taken into new depths of experience. We could only bow down and worship our great God who loves us and heals us, and whose Word is the truth for all time.

Chapter 2

Learning Along the Way

*'He did not do many mighty works there, because of
their unbelief.'*   (Matthew 13:58)

It was not too long before healing became a normal part of
church life. We felt that here at least we were beginning to
approach the spirit of the early church. But all was not plain
sailing. Although many people were healed from a great
variety of diseases, both physical and mental, we also met
many problems. These caused much heart-searching, but
through them we grew in the knowledge of our God.

Some problems sprang from our own selfish natures. It
was very easy to fall into the trap of becoming complacent.
We saw so many acts of healing that we began to expect the
Lord to heal as of right. We treated Him lightly, thinking
that a quick prayer for healing would do the trick. Time and
again, when faced with apparent failure, we had to repent of
this attitude and recall the great scriptural truth that all was
by His grace. We could earn nothing, demand nothing,
claim nothing. Healing was not an automatic right.

In a similar way we fell into the attitude of expecting the
Lord to pander to our selfishness. An incident one holiday
showed us how easy it was to fall into that trap.

We were spending a family holiday at Newquay. It was

great fun and we all enjoyed the Cornish coast. One day we booked a coach trip to Land's End. On the morning of the trip our youngest son was sick after breakfast.

Normally we would have put him to bed for the day. However, we did not want to miss our trip, so we said a quick prayer for him, and set off on the bus, sick child and all. The poor boy was sick most of the day. One of us should have stayed behind with him, but we both wished to go, and expected the Lord to see everything was alright. We tried to misuse His love and power to our own ends, and He will not be manipulated.

Another problem was the lack of response by some who had been healed. There were many occasions when people did not return even to say thank you for their healing. Sometimes second-hand reports would filter back to us that someone we had prayed for was healed, but nothing was heard from the people themselves. We expected to pack the church with people who had experienced the healing power of God, but this did not happen. Once again we showed our ignorance of Scripture. We should have taken seriously the story of the ten lepers (Luke 17:11–19).

We learned, however, that it could be dangerous not to give thanks to the Lord. One parishioner was healed of terrible sores on her hands and feet; another was healed overnight of a curvature of the spine after the laying on of hands with prayer. Neither returned to give thanks to the Lord, and in due course both suffered a recurrence of their troubles, which in at least one case was permanent.

What happened to the nine lepers who did not return to Jesus? We are not told, but the experiences we went through taught us that we must never take the Lord lightly. Rather we should stand in awe of Him, who has in His hands all power of life and death.

The question of why some people are not healed had to be faced. Not everyone we prayed for was healed. Some godly people, for whom we fervently prayed, did not recover, and in some cases died of their illness. We found no ultimate answers to this problem, but we were granted some insights.

One was that we live in an age where there is an atmosphere of unbelief. When Jesus went back to His own home town, people took offence at Him. They knew Him from of old. They knew His family, and they said,

> *'Is not this the carpenter's son? Is not His mother called Mary? And are not His brothers James and Joseph and Simon and Judas? ... Where then did this man get all this?'* (Matthew 13:55, 56)

Matthew tells us that Jesus did not do many mighty works there, because of their unbelief. Mark bluntly tells us, in chapter 6, verse 5, that,

> *'He could do no mighty works there, except that He laid His hands upon a few sick people and healed them. And He marvelled because of their unbelief.'*

The hostility and unbelief of His fellow townsfolk meant the power of Jesus to heal was curtailed. The Incarnate Son of God, in His human self-emptying, could not heal in the face of this atmosphere of scepticism.

In our modern, late twentieth century we live in a similar atmosphere, which is present even in the church. This is bound to have an effect on the healing power which is exercised through the body of Christ.

Another insight was that the Kingdom has not fully come, for Jesus has not returned. Healings and mighty acts are foretastes of what will come, when Jesus returns in power. Therefore we should not expect every one to be healed. It is only as our Lord establishes His Kingdom on earth that we shall see the fullness of His healing power.

We were also made aware that we are living in a spiritual battle. Our fight is not against flesh and blood,

> *'but against the principalities, against the powers, against the world rulers of this present darkness, against the spiritual hosts of wickedness in the heavenly places.'*   (Ephesians 6:12)

Satan *'prowls around like a roaring lion, seeking some one to devour'* (1 Peter 5:8).

Thus he will oppose any ministry which tries to bring the power of God into the world. He will seek to disrupt prayers for healing, he will work to cause setbacks and problems for those who are sick, and discourage those who pray for the sick.

A ministry of healing is a front-line battle against the devil and all his works. I am sure that we gave way on many occasions, even though in Christ we have all the power we need.

Just over a year after being healed of arthritis, Elsie had a dream in which she was unable to hold up her head and shoulders, and could hardly move her legs. As she woke up she found it was reality. Also her eyes were uncoordinated, and her body was full of pain.

As she went to church the following Sunday the pain grew worse. The more she thought of Jesus, the more the pain increased. It was as if she was in a battle. Two days later her minister rebuked the illness in the name of Jesus, and Elsie was back to normal again. All the pain went. She had been subjected to a satanic attack, which would have crippled her had no-one taken a stand in Jesus.

We also know that we made many mistakes. There were times when the Lord called us to make an act of faith, and we failed to respond. Like Peter walking on the water, we looked at external circumstances instead of to Jesus. Our faith failed at the crucial moment, and because of this we let down both the Lord and the sick person. I recall with deep shame an occasion when two church members and myself stood around the bed of a parishioner dying of cancer. We looked at him, said a few words of comfort, and offered a prayer. I left the bedside with a troubled spirit. The Lord had been urging me to tell the man to arise, but I had not the faith to obey. It soon turned out that all three of us had received the same instructions, but there was not one man of faith to be found amongst us. A few days later the patient died. It is good to know that with the Lord there is complete forgiveness through the blood of Jesus, otherwise we would never be able to stand before Him.

On other occasions, we were shown it was not the will of the Lord to heal as we had hoped. He had deeper ways of doing His work.

Joe was a retired miner who was dying of cancer, and lying in great agony. He was the first person we anointed at home. After giving him Communion, we applied the oil with prayer, and as we did so Joe relaxed. All the stress in his body drained away.

'He's going to die now,' I thought in panic.

Joe did not die then, but lived another couple of months, completely free from pain. He lay with a beautiful smile, and the warm glow of the Lord around him. We asked the Lord why Joe was not healed, or why he had not been taken as we anointed him. The answer was that He had taken away the pain, but Joe's wife was not yet willing to let him go. Only when she could release her husband would Joe be taken. She had to be considered as well as Joe. How true it is that the Lord's ways are not our ways. They are far, far higher than ours, and far more loving.

Sometimes we were shown that physical healing was not the best for the person concerned. If they had been physically healed they would have gone off the rails spiritually. Thus it was better, for their eternal salvation, that they should retain their illness. This helped us to put things into the perspective of eternity, and realise that physical healing was not necessarily the be-all and end-all.

At other times an apparent failure turned out to be quite different. Mollie was partially sighted. She came from a family with a history of eye-disease, leading to complete blindness, and was suffering from the same disease.

One Sunday she was anointed, but left the church exactly as she had entered it. No improvement in her sight was noted. She was still partially sighted. We were very upset about this, as we were quite sure we were told to anoint Mollie. Had we done something wrong? Surely the Lord had not let Mollie down? She had a beautiful faith. It is amazing how these questions can rear their ugly heads on these occasions.

Many years later Mollie was visiting the eye specialist. She had been asked to do some card-index filing at work, and was worried that this would damage what remained of her sight.

'There is no trouble,' the doctor told her after he had examined her eyes, 'there is nothing behind but death. You cannot see.'

But Mollie could see; not very well, but no worse than before. Yet medically speaking she was totally blind. We then realised the Lord had done a work of healing the night we anointed Mollie. In some way, best known to Himself, and for His own reasons, He had not restored her sight, but He had arrested its decline.

But there were still other situations where we could not understand why the Lord had not healed. It seemed as though everything was right, and yet no healing was granted.

Does this mean the promise of the Lord to heal is in vain? Or is He selective? Does He have His favourites?

By no means. We recognise that in our earthly state we

see through a glass darkly, and it is only when we see face to face that we shall know the answers to our questions. In the meantime we are called to trust His Word and act upon it, in the sure faith and hope that His purposes do not fail. He is true, and we have seen that He does keep His Word and honour the obedience of His people.

Chapter 3

Blagley

*'I will instruct you and teach you the way you should
go.'* (Psalm 32:8)

Our first view was smoke!

Margaret and I were travelling to Blagley by bus on a fine
March day in 1972, to view the parish. After four years as a
curate in Huddersfield, I had been offered a living of my
own. Across the fields, some two miles away, we saw a
cloud of evil-looking smoke spewing from a bank of tall
chimneys. This turned out to be the outpouring of a
smokeless fuel plant, situated right in the middle of the
village. Until then we had not realised that whilst some
people got fuel without smoke, others got smoke without
fuel. The local coal mine was next door to the plant, and
very soon the pithead gear came into view.

'This looks like it,' I remarked to Margaret, wondering
whatever was in store for us.

As we arrived in Blagley we saw rows and rows of pit
houses. After passing five pubs and a lake, which doubled
up as the beauty spot and the fishing ground of the village,
we alighted at the Market Place. Across the road we saw St
Jude's church. It was flanked by the Vicarage to the left, and
a supermarket to the right. Just behind us, at the bus stop,
was a fish and chip shop.

'At least we are going to be alright for our physical sustenance,' I thought.

We felt that Blagley was the right place for us, and we moved there in July 1972. Little did we know that we were starting a twenty-year ministry in the parish.

I could not help thinking of a remark I had made three years earlier to Dr Eric Treacy, the bishop of Wakefield, who was going to ordain me as priest. After my year as deacon, I was grumbling about the menial tasks a clergyman was expected to do.

'Surely others should do these things, to leave me free for that to which I have been ordained,' I said, rather grandly.

Dr Treacy looked hard at me.

'If you become a Vicar in a South Yorkshire mining parish you will probably have to stoke the boiler as well.'

'I will never become the Vicar of a mining parish, thank you very much,' was my smug, secret thought.

How the Lord lovingly makes us look foolish, and brings us to a position of humility before Him. I had my thoughts, but He had His ways. Here was lesson number one. As with the exiles in Babylon, the Lord had a plan for me. It was a plan *for welfare and not for evil, to give you a future and a hope'* (Jeremiah 29:11). His promise, that He would instruct and teach in the way I should go, was being fulfilled from the start, but I had to learn to surrender my plans, and seek the Lord's way. It took a long time to learn this lesson. My natural arrogance easily came to the fore, and got in the way of the Lord.

On the evening of my induction as Vicar, we had the traditional after-service bun fight in the church hall. After supper I was called upon by the Rural Dean to say a few words. I had not expected this, and had no idea what to say. Apparently I should have thanked all who kept the parish going during the interregnum. Instead, as I looked at the expectant faces before me, and addressed the church for the first time, I said,

'I believe this evening is going to be the start of something great for St Jude's.'

My real meaning was,

'I am here. Just the person you have always wanted. Watch this space. I am going to do a terrific job.'

In many ways it was the start of something great, but not until the Lord had shattered my plans. Like all new vicars I came along with schemes of my own making. I was going to fill the church, and this was the way it was going to be done. I could tell the Lord how to do it. How delighted heaven must be to have me there.

These plans were not necessarily wrong in themselves, but were borne out of an arrogance of spirit which needed humbling. I had to learn that the Lord had His own special agenda for Blagley. My task was not to impose my ideas upon Him, but to carry out His wishes for the church. When I did, things worked out in a wonderful way. But when I ignored, or failed to seek the Lord, things went sadly wrong. The latter was a common occurrence throughout the whole of my ministry. It was easy to be carried away with a bout of enthusiasm and rush on without asking the Lord. Yet His mercy and patience is so wonderful. Every time I fell down He gently restored me. The situation was always turned to good, and we were put on the right path again. How true is the inspired Word,

> *Commit your way to the Lord; trust in Him, and He will act.'* (Psalm 37:5)

We soon found that one of the norms of life in Blagley was to have as little to do with the church as possible. People who went to church were considered different from the rest of mankind. It was a matter of total amazement, and the cause of much scorn and mockery, if someone started going to church. In God's providence this had very beneficial effects. Those who did come to church were, on the whole, very committed people. They had to be, to keep going as Christians. It also made it easy to show the great Bible truth, that once we come to Christ, we are literally brought out of darkness and transferred to His kingdom (Colossians 1:13). There is no half-way stage, no room for lukewarmness. Either we are in or we are out.

The division between the Christians and the non-Christians in the parish came home to me at my first Christmas Eve Eucharist. I was used to the church being packed for this service, and as I processed from the vestry to the sanctuary on Christmas Eve, 1972, I thought our small church would be heaving at the seams. To my amazement, the congregation was exactly the same size as a normal Sunday morning. I was horrified. What had I done wrong? Where was everybody? It dawned on me later that people in Blagley did not go to church unless they went regularly. Hardly anyone came only at Easter and Christmas.

In such an atmosphere we had to work and pray for every single new Christian. This kept us on our toes. There was no room for complacency.

We never grew to large numbers. At the start we had about thirty active members, and over the twenty years we grew to about one hundred and seventy. This is hardly the stuff of church growth manuals, at least as far as numbers are concerned.

As we grew, we reflected the make-up of the area. The Lord blessed us by drawing together a congregation consisting of ordinary working-class people, miners, power station workers, industrial plant operatives, the unemployed and the unemployable, along with the retired. It was a complete microcosm of the working-class community in which we were placed.

We ended up with a good cross-section of ages, from the

very young to the very old, new-born to ninety. We had as
many men as women, except amongst the elderly, where
mortality took its toll of the men first.

The majority of church members were good, old-
fashioned, blunt, Yorkshire folk. Some were blunt to the
point of rudeness. In many ways this was good, because you
knew exactly where you stood. If they did not like the Vicar,
they said so. Often! On the other hand it was quite common
to have upsets in the church, because someone had gone too
far. The Church Annual General Meeting and the Parochial
Church Council meetings were fertile ground for such
happenings.

Our worship was nothing out of the ordinary, just steady
Anglican liturgical worship. We had a Communion service
and an Evensong every Sunday, with a Family Service once
a month, at which the hair could be let down a little. Most
of us did not clap or raise our hands in worship. None of us
danced in the aisles. On the whole we were either formal,
dull or bound, depending on one's point of view.

Unlike most churches, we drew a larger congregation in
the evening than in the morning. I could never work out the
reason why, unless beds in Blagley were more comfortable
than elsewhere.

As a matter of deliberate policy we tried to model our
church life on the Scriptures. We accepted the Bible as the
true Word of God, and believed it could be wholly relied
upon to show us God's ways and commands.

We believed the world was created in six days of twenty-
four hours, and that God rested on the seventh day; that
Jonah was swallowed by a big fish; and that Balaam's ass
really did speak. We accepted without doubt the miracles of
both the Old and New Testaments. We had no difficulty in
believing the accounts of the Virgin Birth and the bodily
Resurrection of our Lord. We looked for His Second
Coming, and prayed that it would be soon.

We held that if we sought to obey God's Word in all things, then He would act. And this was so. As we tried to follow the Scriptures, usually imperfectly and always in trepidation, He did things which were beyond our expectations and our wildest dreams. When His people seek to obey, God is indeed faithful.

All this was to His glory alone. I often marvelled that our working-class Christians were so wise in the ways of the Lord. Yet it was a wisdom given by the Spirit: it was all His doing.

In these days when a simple belief in the Bible is treated with contempt, even by many within the churches, it is necessary to remind ourselves that

> *'all Scripture is inspired by God and profitable for teaching, for reproof, for correction, and for training in righteousness.'* (2 Timothy 3:16)

Once we abandon this biblical rock, both our personal Christian lives, and our church life, fall to pieces. But if we come to the Word, trusting it as God's truth, we are built up in His glory, and will not be shaken.

Chapter 4

New Lives

'Therefore, if any one is in Christ, he is a new creation; the old has passed away, behold, the new has come.'
(2 Corinthians 5:17)

'Hello Cath, where are you rushing off to?'

Cath was a well dressed, twice married lady in her forties. Although we had met on several occasions, I did not know her very well. She was almost flying down the street.

'I'm going to the solicitors, to get a divorce,' she said.

'Hold on,' I replied, 'you don't need a solicitor. You need Jesus. Come to church with me, and let's pray about it.'

She came into the church, and after a bit of talking, we knelt at the altar rail. There and then Cath gave her life to the Lord. I don't know which of us was the more surprised. But from that moment on Cath was gloriously converted, and grew into a radiant Christian woman. She did not go to the solicitors. Obviously the Holy Spirit had been working unseen, and unknown, upon Cath's soul for a long time. He used a time of crisis to bring her to a new birth, and a new life.

Jesus said, *'I came that they may have life, and have it abundantly'* (John 10:10:), and the whole New Testament witnesses to the new life that comes through believing in

Him. In common with so many churches we experienced this truth in those who turned to Christ. Their lives were literally transformed.

Joan was beset by fears. She had great difficulty in going out of her house, even to the shops. A trip to nearby Doncaster was out of the question. One evening she came to an evangelistic house meeting for adults. Only the Lord knows how she got there, and what went on in her spirit, but she was brought to the Lord. Over the months her fears withered away, or she was given grace to cope with them. It was not too long before the Lord gave her a burden for children. She taught in the Sunday School, and has been an inspiration to many children over the years. To see the new Joan, glowing with love, teaching the children about her Lord, and comparing her with the old Joan, was to see a living example of the new life that is in Christ.

Johnnie and Enid were miner and wife. Their little daughter, Natalie, had been to church on a school visit. She asked,

'Why don't we go to church?'

They did, were converted, and are today serving the Lord in a full-time capacity.

Janet and Gwen came to our Evening service on three consecutive Sundays after the death of Janet's mother. It was part of our local tradition that members of the deceased's family appeared at church for one or more Sundays after the funeral. Normally we never saw them again until the next bereavement. The difference with Janet and Gwen was that they never stopped coming. Those visits brought them to Jesus, who turned their lives upside down. In due time, after much prayer, their husbands followed, and they too became children of God.

Sam was unemployed and lived alone. He knew many of the members at St Jude's, and like others before him, one day drifted into a church service. Within a few weeks he was kneeling at the altar rail, giving his whole life to Christ. He was reborn, as a son of God, and is now part of a loving family.

Paul was a psychiatric nurse. His mother had recently become a Christian, and he went with her to a Billy Graham Mission meeting at Sheffield in 1985. He came back a Christian man, with new attitudes and a new outlook on life. Instead of being a caring nurse, he was now a caring Christian nurse, bringing the presence of Jesus into his work.

Alf suffered from deep mental problems. He went to the same Billy Graham Mission meeting, and as the call went out for people to come forward, he stood up in his seat, and shouted to all the world,

'I'm coming, Billy.'

He raced to the front. His wife, Laura, went with him, or rather followed behind him, and together, after years of struggle and upsets, they gave their lives to the Lord. The mental problems were still there, but from now on Alf had a new power, a new Christian wife, and new friends to support and help him through them.

Polly, who had turned to drink; Russ and Jean, who came to the Lord through their daughter's illness; Elaine who had marriage problems; Henry, who suffered inward torments; Audrey, who looked at a friend who had recently turned to Christ and wished she had got the same, were all people in the area who came to the Lord, and found a new life in Him.

There were very many more, some of whom we shall meet in the following pages. All were living examples of the biblical truth that those who turn to Christ become new creatures, filled with the heavenly life that He alone can bring.

It goes without saying that **we** converted no-one. Conversion is the work of the Holy Spirit, who convicts us of our sins, and opens our eyes to a Saviour. Our task was to proclaim Jesus, to placard Jesus, as it says in Galatians 3:1, and the Holy Spirit did the rest. As we tried to show the Jesus who is given to us in the Scriptures, and be true to the Word of God, so we saw a healthy newness of life flood into the church. Men and women were set free from all sorts of worldly and demonic problems, and there was great joy.

Not only were people brought in from the outside, but faithful church members suddenly came into a new spiritual life. After spending three years in the parish, I received a letter which speaks for itself. It said,

> 'Praise the Lord for three years of Great Awakening, and because now for me Jesus is REAL and ALIVE and ALL that I want or need.'

We believe that all this happened because we sought to be true to the Scriptures. We tried to preach the gospel as it is, and not trim the message until it is diluted of all spiritual power. Even though the Scriptures go against so much of what our world holds dear, there is within them a tremendous spiritual power to change lives. A gospel which is altered to conform to modern day fads and presuppositions has no power. It is only the truth of God, as we are given it in the Bible, that brings about that newness of life in Christ.

Chapter 5

The Power to Live

'Be filled with the Spirit.'   (Ephesians 5:18)

Our converts at Blagley were, like all new Christians, rough-hewn, imperfect people. Many had undergone terrible experiences in their previous non-Christian lives. They were filled with wrong attitudes, and were unaware, in many cases, of the difference between right and wrong. It was not uncommon for our new sheep to tell the Vicar about their winnings at the previous night's Bingo. Adult confirmation groups would often hear what someone had read in their horoscope that day.

It did not take us long to realise, that when someone came to Christ the hard work then began. The new-born Christian had to be nourished, encouraged and disciplined, so that he could grow in Christ, with the ultimate aim of presenting him pure and spotless before the Lord.

Many clergy find this the hardest task of all. I do not think I was the only one who sometimes cherished a secret dream of becoming a travelling evangelist. I could then preach Christ, see people converted, and move on, leaving someone else to pick up the pieces.

This shows I did not understand, or believe, the teachings of the Scriptures about the Holy Spirit. We are clearly told that the Holy Spirit ever seeks to clean up the lives of Christians. He works to bring us to holiness and perfection, so that we become Christlike people. After we have been saved, we are renewed in the Holy Spirit (Titus 3:5), and by the Spirit we are to put to death the deeds of the body (Romans 8:13).

One morning there was a ringing of the Vicarage front door-bell. On the doorstep stood Bella, trembling all over and looking awful.

'Come in, and sit down,' I said. 'What can I do for you?'

'I want to give up smoking,' she agonised, 'I know it is wrong for a Christian to smoke, and I really want to come off. I have tried, but I cannot do it. Please help me.'

'Now what do I say?' I groaned inwardly. 'Lord, please help me.'

I had no medication or humanly devised plan to help Bella. Nor could I give her the strength she so obviously needed. She had been smoking for years, and was well and truly hooked. In the end I blurted out,

'The Holy Spirit has shown you this problem in your life. Trust Him and He will give you the strength to solve it.'

I must confess that, at the time, it sounded like a cop-out. Yet, in a bungling way, it was the right answer. The Holy Spirit had indeed convicted Bella about her smoking. I had never preached or taught about it. Thus the Holy Spirit would give her the strength to come off.

The Holy Spirit will bring us to that holiness of life, without which no one can see God. Of course, we have to co-operate with Him, and allow Him to do His work. We must not quench Him, or oppose Him. But in the end it is His work, and His alone.

It was a great joy to see our new Christians seeking to open themselves to the influence of the Holy Spirit. Gradually they became aware of the truth as it is in Christ, concerning all sorts of practical issues like divorce, gambling, and the occult. They were then given the power to cope with these things as they affected their own lives. Some who were bound by horoscopes were enabled to stop reading them. Many gave up all sorts of gambling. This was not by their own efforts, because it meant breaking the habit of a lifetime. It was solely by the power of the Spirit.

Jesus promises that the Holy Spirit will lead us into all truth. We saw the Spirit doing just that amongst our church members, and producing His fruits in these new, reborn Christians. As a sculptor takes a rough block of stone and slowly chisels it into a beautiful shape, so the Holy Spirit took these rough Christians, and slowly crafted them into beautiful people.

As well as being rough-hewn, our new Christians were powerless. Or, at least, they thought they were. Inferiority complexes were endemic in the area. They were shown in such expressions as,

'I'm only a miner' (or 'miner's wife');

'I was no good at school'; or

'I only come from a working class family.'

The very thought of 'doing something in the church' was enough to make them run a thousand miles. I could hardly blame them, because I myself took a long time to accept the Lord's call to the ministry.

Paul, writing to the Christians at Corinth, says,

> *'For consider your call, brethren; not many of you were wise according to worldly standards, not many were powerful, not many were of noble birth.'*
>
> (1 Corinthians 1:26)

We could have said the same for our Christians at Blagley, except we would have had to replace the words 'not many' by 'none'. Yet as the church grew, there was an ever-increasing need for more people to become involved in ministry, and all sorts of service. Unlike most churches we had no reservoir of middle-class leadership, so we had to use those whom the Lord had given us. This was where the Holy Spirit came into His own, as it were.

The Bible teaches that the Spirit gives gifts of power. These are supernatural gifts, given to whom He wills. They are not natural endowments. We are not born with them. They are gifts of grace. The qualifications for receiving them are a belief in Jesus and an openness to ask for, and to receive, all that the Holy Spirit wishes to give. They are then given irrespective of position, intellect and worldly ability.

Their whole purpose is to enable Christians to serve God, by bringing His power into the life of the church. Therefore, we argued, if our folk were open to receive the gifts of the Spirit, we had no need to worry about lack of leadership. The Holy Spirit would enable them to overcome their fears and complexes, and give us a powerful, Spirit-filled body of people, who would use their gifts in the service of the Lord.

Two barriers had to be overcome before this could happen. One was to realise that the gifts of the Spirit are available today. The other was a re-run of the inferiority complex. This time it was,

'I cannot expect the Holy Spirit to give His gifts to me. I am only a working man. In any case, I am not good enough.'

So we had to show that the Holy Spirit does give His gifts to miners, as well as to ministers. In fact the Spirit delights to pour Himself out on all flesh, on the old and young alike, on menservants and maidservants (Acts 2:17).

We learned that the Greek word for the gifts of the Spirit is *'charismata'*, which means 'birthday present'. As we give birthday presents to those whom we love, so the Spirit gives gifts to those who live within the love of God. We do not expect people to earn a birthday present, so we cannot earn these gifts.

Once these scriptural facts were understood, the barriers came down. People started to pray for baptism of the Holy Spirit, and we saw a steady revealing of the gifts within the congregation. They appeared in all sorts of ways, and I was constantly receiving telephone calls such as,

'Peter, I spoke in tongues last night. Guess where? In the bath!' or

'Our Andrea's hamster died last night. We found it dead in the cage this morning. I took it in my hands and prayed, "Lord, if it be Thy will, let this hamster come back to life." I couldn't believe it. It just ran off my hands. It took us ages to catch it.' or,

'Beryl was ill last night. I felt the urge to lay my hands on her and pray for her healing. It was wonderful. I felt a burning sensation in my hands, and she is better now.'

As the different gifts were given to church members, we found that they were naturally used within the personal and home life of the Christian. It was harder to learn how to use them in a church situation. There were times when we misused the gifts, and times when we failed to use them because our faith ran out. Yet the Holy Spirit gently taught us along the way, and was more than patient with our failings.

Most difficult of all was the use of the gifts within the worshipping life of the church. People did not speak in tongues or prophesy in church services, although some prayed quietly in tongues during worship, and many words of prophecy were given which people brought to me later. It seemed easier to use the gifts openly at prayer meetings, rather than in our ordered Anglican worship. However, the elders were often given words of knowledge and wisdom for those being anointed for healing.

Above all, the gifts of the Spirit were for the upbuilding of the church. As different members exercised varied gifts, so the church was encouraged, and grew towards the fullness of Christ. Thus some were given gifts of discernment, which were used in ministering to those in need. Others had gifts of healing, which were used in a quiet unspectacular way as they came across sick people. Still others were given words of wisdom in difficult situations, and others had a powerful gift of casting out demons.

A personal experience of the effectiveness of the gifts was given at a time when I was feeling a failure. I do not know why I felt like this. It was probably self-pity. Whilst walking on the street I met a very gifted church member, another Margaret. She looked straight at me and said,

'Peter, the Lord tells me you feel a failure.'

At that moment such feelings disappeared. I realised that the Lord knew all about my situation, and that I was safe in His hands. Such is the power of a spoken, Spirit-filled word.

Above all, the Holy Spirit brought His love amongst us. Love is the fruit of the Spirit, and in some special way, He brought this love in large measure to our church. Paul rejoices that,

> *'God's love has been poured into our hearts through the Holy Spirit which He has given us.'* (Romans 5:5)

and we could similarly rejoice.

If I had to give the one distinguishing mark of the church at Blagley it would be love. There were many things that were wrong in our church. We could, and should, have done many things better. Many ideas and projects went wrong. At times our services were a shambles. People were insecure, weak and quarrelsome. But over and above all, and permeating the whole life of the church, was that supernatural love of God which only the Spirit brings. We shall describe in a later chapter how this love was practically shown during the 1984 coal strike, but it is enough to say here that God's love was truly in our midst.

People still had rows, but they learned to say sorry. Older church members were sometimes suspicious of new members, but they quickly learned to accept them and love them in the Lord. Some members had grievances which had their roots in the dim and distant past. Yet the Holy Spirit poured His healing love even into such situations.

On arriving at church for the first time, Pauline saw Ben. Immediately her mind flashed back some twenty years when she had been a disruptive girl living in the same street as Ben. At that time Ben had frightened Pauline by shouting at her, and was definitely someone to be avoided. Her next thought was to get out fast. Then Ben saw Pauline, and remembered the naughty girl who had caused so much disruption. They looked at each other, smiled, and all was well in the Lord.

We had couples joining us whose marriages were almost finished. The Holy Spirit poured God's love into those marriages and mended them. There were many occasions of grief and personal tragedy within the church. The Spirit of love simply led people to hug each other, and offer what practical help they could. It was all spontaneous. There was no need to tell people to do it. The love of God had been poured in by the Spirit.

Even people outside the church noted the love that was in our midst, and many, on entering the church for the first time, remarked on the almost tangible atmosphere of love. There were many occasions, especially after worship, when you could almost touch the love. A frequent sight at the end of a service was small groups of people praying for someone who was in need. That was truly the love which the Spirit had poured out amongst us. We often said that if the love went from the church we would be left with nothing.

This was just as Scripture says it should be, and we were privileged to see, yet again, biblical truth vindicated in our midst. For that we can only give glory and thanks to God.

Chapter 6

In All Things by Prayer

'Pray constantly.'   (1 Thessalonians 5:17)

I was walking past the church gates one evening about 4 o'clock, when Eric grabbed me. He was on his way home from the pub, and had obviously been loosened by drink, which probably explains why he had the courage to speak to the Vicar.

'I don't believe in God,' was his opening gambit.

'OK,' I replied.

'But one day I'll come into your church.'

'Why don't you come now?'

'What, now?'

'Yes, why not? There is no need to be scared. There will be nobody there apart from you and me.'

We walked slowly together up the church path. I was not sure whether we would make it into the church, or whether Eric would bottle out at the last minute. We got inside, and I showed Eric the building. It only took a couple of minutes, as there was not a lot to see.

'Can I say a prayer for you?' I asked.

Eric looked at me and burst into tears.

'Say a prayer for my dog. He is suffering from cancer. I'm taking him to the vet tomorrow to have him put down.'

That, of course, was what Eric had wanted all along. So I said a prayer for the dog, and one for the owner as well.

Many weeks later I came across Eric in the street. He looked hard at me.

'Vicar,' he said, 'my dog is better. I took him to the vet and there was no cancer.'

Eric was not a member of our church, nor, I suspect of any other. Yet at some deep level he realised his need of prayer. His life was far from what it should have been, and it was obvious that drink played too great a part in the daily routine. But underneath there was a crying out for God; an urge to make contact with Him to pour out his heart before Him. Eric would not have expressed it like that. He would probably never have expressed it at all. But in times of need, almost by instinct, he turned to God in prayer.

The Scriptures are full of people of all shapes and sizes who do that very thing. One of the great themes of the Bible is the need to pray. Jesus tells us that we *'ought always to pray and not lose heart'* (Luke 18:1). He undergirds this with many promises about the results of prayer. He says,

> *'Ask, and it will be given you; seek, and you will find; knock, and it will be opened to you.'*   (Luke 11:9)

Yet for most of us, it is more attractive to do some practical task, than go to a prayer meeting or service of intercession. When we meet together at Sunday services, we prefer to sing hymns and choruses rather than spend time in real intercessory prayer. If we take a dispassionate look at our services we soon find that intercession takes up a very small proportion of the time.

Jesus never said, 'Do and you shall receive.' It was always *'Ask.'*

The early Christians also had problems with prayer, for we find James telling them,

'You do not have, because you do not ask.' (James 4:2)

We have to ask our Lord for everything. When we come to Him in prayer and lay our needs and requests before Him, then He acts. It is as if a floodgate is opened; the power of the Lord comes pouring through.

We are told,

'The prayer of a righteous man has great power in its effects.' (James 5:16)

And even if there be but two or three together, Jesus is present (Matthew 18:20). The agreement of two on earth means it shall be done (Matthew 18:19). Jesus knows our every weakness, and in love He encourages us to get on our knees and pray.

Despite knowing all these promises and words of encouragement, we were slow at St Jude's when it came to prayer. There were many times when we should have met together for prayer but failed to do so. We preferred to rely upon our worldly wisdom, and left aside the wisdom that comes from God.

Mischief Night, November 4th, was always a great event in the Blagley social calendar. It was that night when householders stuffed old rags in their letter boxes to prevent fireworks being pushed through; when removable gates were taken off their hinges and stored in the garden shed; and when the police were extra vigilant.

The 1984 proceedings were different. Mischief turned to positive evil. The coal strike was in its eighth month. Things were getting desperate and feelings running very high. Violence was threatened between the local pickets and the police. The game of the season in the school yards was Police and Strikers. Cops and Robbers had long since disappeared. Stealing what little coal could be found was a full-time industry. Marriages were under strain and people were at breaking point.

Along came November 4th, and things boiled over. It was total mayhem. Gangs of youths, and children younger than ten, roamed the streets. Windows were broken, and cars were sprayed with paint. Elderly residents were threatened with death messages sprayed on their doors. People stayed inside through sheer fear. And the church slept. We did nothing. We knew the situation was tense but we did not even bother to take it to the Lord. We never prayed.

Thankfully, it was a lesson learned. There was a strong possibility that the following year's mischief would be even worse, so note was made to do better. We were also reminded that Hallow E'en came a few days before Mischief Night. This was another of the great social festivals of the area, when all manner of occult abominations were practised. We realised that the one led to the other. Perhaps the demons let loose at Hallow E'en incited the younger members of the community to violence at Mischief Night.

So, just to be sure, we had prayer meetings in church on both days in 1985. We prayed for protection against demonic forces at Hallow E'en, and we prayed the night before Mischief Night that all would be quiet. We did not pray in any special way, but came before God and asked Him,

'Please, Lord, bind the demons,'

'Protect those who play with the occult,' and

'Father, please let it be quiet on Mischief Night.'

And, praise God, it was quiet. In the villages all around us there was great violence. It was as if the powers of evil were trying to whip up feelings to make 1985 even worse than 1984. But in Blagley there was total peace. It had not been so quiet for years. The Holy Spirit had moved into the situation in response to our prayers, and had restrained the violence. We even heard reports of children being kept indoors that night. This was something unknown in our parish.

'Ask, and it will be given you.'

How we rejoiced. Yet we were being reminded of something we had forgotten, for we had been taught, at a very early stage in our ministry, that prayer would bind and restrain evil.

Angela was one of the first new members of our church. Judith her next door neighbour was definitely not a Christian. Like most people, her trust was in the things of this world; yet she was without peace in her life. Angela sought to witness to her, but to no avail.

One day Judith announced that she was going to see a fortune-teller. Angela warned her not to go. It was dangerous. God said such things were wrong. But Judith insisted. She had made an appointment, and the fortune-teller was expecting her at half-past two that afternoon.

Angela rang up the Vicar.

'What shall I do?' she asked in panic.

'Pray, and get some other people to pray with you,' I replied.

So this was done. In the early afternoon, a number of people were praying that Judith would be protected from the evil of the fortune-teller. I am not sure what we expected, but when Judith returned home she was dumbfounded, or gobsmacked as we would have put it. As the fortune-teller opened her door and saw Judith, she let out a shriek, and slammed the door in her face. We do not know what the clairvoyant saw, but we can be sure that Judith was surrounded by the protection of the Lord.

It would be nice to say that Judith became a Christian after this; it would also be nice to relate that we never forgot the power of prayer from then onwards. Sadly, we can say neither. Judith left the district without coming to the Lord; and we soon forgot what had happened. I once used to wonder how the Israelites could forget the mighty acts of God in Egypt. Now I know, and can only marvel at our Lord's patience with a forgetful and unfaithful people.

We also found that prayer would bind the rebellious hearts of Christians, and bring the Lord's people together in one mind and one spirit.

Anyone who has served on a Parochial Church Council, or its equivalent, will know all about squabbles, rows and upsets. A typical Church Council meeting can go something like this.

A matter will come up for consideration. The Vicar will say a word of introduction, not daring to lay down too strict a line of his own, but hoping in his heart that all will pass off smoothly, without any disturbance.

Then the topic goes for general discussion. Mr Jones speaks strongly for the resolution. Mrs Shaw speaks equally strongly against it.

'We have tried this before, and it did not work. Mr Jones is only a new member of the church, and will not remember.' (New, in this context, can mean anything up to thirty or forty years.)

Miss Smith backs Mr Jones. She is an even newer member, and is keen to move forward. Mrs Tinker, who has been on the Church Council since the war, recounts the things of the past, and pours cold water on the proposal, and on those who support it.

'We have seen people come and go at this church,' she says with meaning. 'They are always suggesting new ideas, but they never work. We should continue to do as we have always done.'

Other members are drawn in to an increasingly tense situation, and for a while the purpose of the discussion is lost altogether as members score points against each other. Finally, in a vain attempt to cool things down the Vicar gets in with another word.

'We have had a full and frank discussion of the issues involved,' (which he knows is not true). 'Let's put the matter to the vote.'

The vote is taken by a show of hands. The Council is equally divided – ten for and ten against. It is up to the Vicar to give his chairman's casting vote. All eyes are upon him, and he knows that whichever way he votes he will alienate, and perhaps lose, some members.

This sort of thing happens at countless Church meetings up and down the land. We had our share at Blagley. There were many mornings when, after a bad meeting and an even worse night, I had to ring round various members to try to pour oil on troubled waters. I was once advised that a Vicar should never resign on a Monday morning or after a Church Council meeting!

Thankfully, the Lord worked through our situation. He knew what we were like, and He took us from the very point where we were, and gently, but firmly moved us forward.

He first made us realise that rows and upsets are not what He desires in any church meeting. They are against His will. Having learned that, we tried earnestly to do something about it. A prayer was written, in which we told the Lord we were sorry for the hurts we had caused, and that we would seek at all times to be one with each other. This prayer was said at the start of each meeting, and I believe it helped us to see our position before the Lord.

We then saw that our Church Council meetings were really secular meetings under a Christian name. We did not approach each meeting with prayer. Of course, we had an opening prayer, but then we passed quickly on to what we considered to be the real business of the meeting. There was little sense that we were the Lord's people, seeking to do His will.

We tackled this problem in a number of ways. The opening prayer was extended into a short service. We also slowly and painfully learned that sometimes we needed to stop discussions and turn to prayer in the middle of the meeting. It was amazing how often an insoluble problem was solved after we had prayed about it.

But above all we were shown that we should be of one mind on every issue that came before us. The Apostle Paul tells us to be of one mind and one spirit. He also makes the astounding declaration,

> *'We have the mind of Christ.'*   (1 Corinthians 2:16)

We reckoned that this should be seen, even in the nitty gritty of the Church Council meeting. If we have the mind of Christ, then we should see any issue according to His way of thinking. This meant surrendering our human thoughts and ideas to Him, and seeking His mind about everything that came before us. If what Paul said was right, and if we truly had Christ's mind, then we should all be brought to the same conclusion. The mind of Christ is not split or divided.

So we reasoned, and in a mad moment of faith, we resolved that we would take no decisions on any matter, until the Church Council was of one mind.

This meant that every member had to seriously and prayerfully consider each question that arose. There could be no passengers on the Council, for everyone had a vital role to play. It also meant that no votes would ever be taken. This delighted me, for I had long noticed that every time a church meeting had a vote on an issue, those who lost the vote felt hurt and rejected, and often became hard of heart. If something we had voted on did not work, the attitude of 'told you so' raised its ugly head. Surely this was not the way of God.

We realised that we could get to the state of making no decisions at all, but this did not happen. There were times when we found great difficulty in finding our Lord's mind, and there were times when we all got it wrong. We had to learn to submit our wills to His perfect Will. Yet He did bring us to one mind on so many things, and we learned that if we prayed, it would be as He said. We asked, we received; we knocked, and doors were opened to us.

The same manner of working also applied in a later stage of our growth, when we had elders. As an eldership, we sought the Lord's mind, which we believed was ours in Christ.

How many church divisions would be avoided if we took the words of Scripture at face value and sought to follow them literally? Jesus, our High Priest, prays we shall be one. This is a practical oneness, which has to be realised in and through the everyday life of the church. Only prayer, which holds to the truth of the Word, can bring us to that state.

Another challenge was put before us. If we believed the Scriptures to be true and relevant, we ought to pray before appointing people to positions of service in the church. Jesus spent the whole night in prayer before choosing twelve Apostles from His many followers (Luke 6:12), and the church at Antioch were at prayer when Barnabas and Saul were called to missionary work (Acts 13:1-3).

We did not find it easy to wait for guidance. It was hard to stop relying on human judgement. When we needed a Sunday School teacher, for example, our natural reaction was to look around the congregation and wonder,

'Who is good with children? Oh yes, she might be alright. I'll ask her.'

Or, if we were stuck, we would ask for volunteers. Now we had to pray,

'Lord, we are short of a Sunday School teacher. Please show us who You choose to do this work.'

This taught us patience. Although our prayers were answered, it was not always at once. Our natural impatience had to be disciplined.

Sometimes the answer was not what we expected. Either the person chosen was not the one **we** would have picked, or we were told that the Lord had chosen nobody. On some occasions our attention was directed to a different need in the church, which the Lord showed was more important. There were also times when we listened to our own inclinations rather than to the Lord. Yet we genuinely sought His will, and we believed He would rectify our errors.

Despite these mistakes, we had the assurance that the right person was doing the right task. The round peg was in the round hole. This gave everybody security and confidence. When things go wrong in Christian ministry, the tempter quickly whispers, 'You should not be doing this work. You are not the right person for it.' At these times it is a great strength to know that the church leadership only appoints through prayer.

This scriptural approach also saved us from the curse of volunteers. It is a sin of the flesh, that when we see some need in the church, we rush forward to offer ourselves, with great enthusiasm. Although we are zealous, we do not pray about it, and we end up out of our Lord's will. Many Christians have collapsed under the strain of doing a task which was not meant for them in the first place.

The same approach also covered a cowardly Vicar from volunteers who came from outside the church, and who were often sent by the other side. As we were seeking to understand the healing ministry, I was approached by someone I had never met, who offered herself as a healer. The suggestion was that this person could come along to our healing services, and help me in the laying on of hands.

I was terrified. I sensed something demonic, but found it hard to put my finger on it. Many wise leaders would have been able to do so, but I was a learner, and very green. But I did say,

'Thank you very much, but our policy is always to pray about tasks that people do in the church. I will pray about it and let you know if it is the will of the Lord.'

And that was the end of that. A little battle had been won. Later I found out that the person was involved in spiritism.

From this I realised that non-church members could not be used in any category of church life. Those who serve in the body of Christ must be part of that body.

Prayer is the greatest need of the church. Through seeking God we are led into great peace and stability. Paul tell us to

> *'have no anxiety about anything, but in everything by prayer and supplication with thanksgiving let your requests be made known to God.'* (Philippians 4:6)

Then he makes the great promise,

> *'And the peace of God, which passes all understanding, will keep your hearts and your minds in Christ Jesus.'* (Philippians 4:7)

Chapter 7

Signs and Wonders

'Thou art the God who workest wonders.'

(Psalm 77:14)

It was crisis time at St Jude's!

We had been there long enough for the newness to wear off. The honeymoon was well and truly over. The church was full of gossip and back-biting, and these were threatening its life. I found this very frightening. I had never come across such a situation before. How do you deal with undercurrents and cross-currents, the innuendoes and rumours which go to make up a typical church-splitting situation?

It was obviously time to speak out or get out, and having nowhere else to go, it must be speak out. So, in much fear and trembling, a sermon, which was really the reading of the Riot Act, was prepared for the following Sunday.

'How will they take it?'

'How many will walk out and leave the church?'

'Will anybody take any notice anyway?'

All these sorts of thoughts went through my mind in the days before Sunday. I need not have worried. The Lord was in control.

On Saturday evening Margaret went to a performance of

the Elijah, and came back with a message from the Lord. During the concert she was told that angels would be protecting me on Sunday. She was thrilled about this at the concert. But on her way home she felt less and less sure of herself, and all the usual negative thoughts came flooding in. Was it really a message from the Lord? Did she make it up?

On arrival at the Vicarage the desire to pass on the message had evaporated. Yet she did tell me, from the safety of halfway up the stairs.

'Don't worry about tomorrow, the angels will look after you,' she shouted, and then dashed out of the way.

In my lack of faith I frankly took little notice. My mind was too occupied with my own troubles to listen to the Lord.

The Riot Act was read the next day, and I forgot about the angels. But not for long. About two days later I heard a strange report. Joan had seen two angels hovering over the altar whilst I was preaching. She was ecstatic about it.

'They were beautiful,' she kept on saying, 'Just beautiful.'

It was then, of course, that I remembered Margaret's words. Being of a suspicious nature I checked up to see if Joan knew what Margaret had told me. But there was no collusion. The Lord had spoken and then confirmed His word in such a way that we could not doubt.

What a glorious and wonderful Father we have. How great and mysterious are His ways. From then on I had no doubt about the reality of angels.

Over the years other church members saw angels, and occasionally even heard heavenly voices singing in the church. Jack, an ex-soldier, once told me with tears in his eyes, that during Evensong he had heard the heavenly choir.

'Are you sure it wasn't us?' I foolishly asked.

'Oh no. It was beautiful,' came the reply.

This was not an intended comment on our attempts to sing. Jack had been transported, for a brief moment, into the heavenly realms. It sometimes seemed that the distance between ourselves and our heavenly inheritance was so very small. Heaven was almost tangible.

We were privileged to see many signs and wonders. This was not something we were expecting, or looking for. Again, our ignorance of Scripture was shown up. In the early church, God bore witness to the gospel message of salvation, *'by signs and wonders and various miracles and by gifts of the Holy Spirit'* (Hebrews 2:4).

Jesus promised that this would happen (Mark 16:17, 18). Jesus is the same, yesterday, today and forever. His promises stand for ever. So we should expect to see signs and wonders today, provided we seek to proclaim the message of eternal life, through Him.

Not only did the Lord grant supernatural protection in time of need, but He also had His ways of covering up our mistakes and lack of faith.

One Christmas we rashly decided, without prayer, to hold a Christingle service. Every child, we decreed, would receive a Christingle. Therefore we had to guess how many children would be present. We settled on a figure of sixty, expecting it to be an over-estimate. I thought twenty to twenty-five would be more likely, but it would cause great hurt if even one child left the church without a Christingle.

So we purchased sixty oranges, sixty red candles, and all the other materials needed. We knew exactly how many oranges and candles we had bought. After all, they cost money and we had to be careful. A day or two before the service we panicked and bought some satsumas. We did not make them into Christingles, but they would be better than nothing if more than sixty children turned up.

The church was packed on the evening of the service, and seemed to be crawling with children. Just to add to the fun, a group of Cub Scouts turned up unannounced. It is difficult to describe our emotions at that moment. We had never seen the church full before. Yet all those children...!

Towards the end of the service the youngsters came forward to receive their Christingles. It seemed like a football crowd. There was a constant stream coming with bright eyes and open hands, whilst all the time our box of precious Christingles was being used up.

The choir were singing Christmas carols, the Vicar was almost tearing his hair, and the two people who had made the Christingles were counting as the children came forward. In the front row of the choir were five children. They also began to panic.

'Save some for us, Mr Noble,' they pleaded.

One of the Christingle makers was standing behind me, passing Christingles forward, whilst I put them into eager hands, wondering when we would run out. Finally the row of children dried up, and we had just five Christingles remaining for the young choir members. The last child got the last Christingle. I went back to my stall, thankfully said the final prayers and announced the closing carol. We had just made it.

After the service Hilary, another of the Christingle makers said to me,

'Do you know how many children came forward tonight?'

It did not take a mathematician to work that one out.

'Just sixty,' I replied with great authority.

'No, it was eighty.'

'How could it have been?'

'Well it was,' said Hilary, 'but as the children were coming up I thought if the Lord could make five loaves and two fishes go round, He can make sure we are alright with Christingles.'

We found out afterwards that other people in the congregation had been of the same mind, and had prayed that we would have enough to go round.

There is no doubt the Lord worked a miracle for us that night. Yet it was all so natural and loving. God showed how great is His love, and how He is able to do far more than we can even ask or think.

We quickly learned that signs and wonders are not given by the Lord for show or display. They always have some practical and spiritual purpose. It was tempting to seek signs for worldly entertainment. There was often the desire within us to see something spectacular. This was what the Pharisees wanted when they asked Jesus for a sign. It was also one of the wilderness temptations which our Lord had to overcome. If He had wished, He could have thrown Himself down from the Temple and the angels would have protected Him. Yet such a feat would not have led anyone to repentance and new life.

A couple of years after the 1984 coal strike the Blagley Gala was resurrected. This was a village affair, which started in the morning with a procession of floats, led by the Colliery brass band. The afternoon was spent on the Miner's Welfare cricket field with games, side stalls, food and drink. It seemed right to have a visible church presence at the new Gala, so we organised a Sunday School float and a church bookstall.

The Sunday School teachers met to decide how to organise the float. They were apprehensive, as it was something they had never done before. Gwen, one of the teachers, spoke up.

'I have seen the float in a dream,' she said. 'It must be about heaven. The children are to be dressed in white. There must be a cross, which has to be high and lifted up. Everybody must be able to see it.'

Gwen was respected as a very godly lady. This was not something she would be making up. So the attitude of all present was,

'Right Gwen. You're in charge. Tell us what to do.'

Whilst other people set about making white clothes for the children, Gwen started to make the cross. She cut a cross out of a cardboard box picked up from the super-market. She wanted to paint the figure of Jesus on the cross, but felt inadequate. So she just covered the cardboard with streaks of brown and gold paint.

When the paint had dried, her husband, Jack, exclaimed, 'Gwen, you've painted Jesus on the cross after all.'

'No I haven't,' she replied.

'Well, He's there. I can see Him.'

And sure enough, the paint had dried in such a way that a figure of Jesus could be seen. Once the cross was placed on the float, the figure of our Lord was even clearer, and as the Gala procession wound its way round the village streets Christ crucified was lifted up for all to see. It was the outstanding feature of the procession, and many onlookers were moved by the sight.

Our experience of signs and wonders took us into far deeper waters than we imagined possible. One of the signs which Jesus said would accompany believers was,

'In my name they will cast out demons.' (Mark 16:17)

This created a problem. We knew that Jesus had cast out demons, and that His followers in the early church had also been used in this way. We believed theoretically, that since the Spirit of Jesus was present in His church, we also ought to see demons cast out. The difficulty was translating theory into practice. There was a great need for this ministry in Blagley, for it was riddled with demonic forces. Spiritism was rife, and ouija boards were commonplace, even amongst school children. Witchcraft was also prevalent in the area. All around was a swirling force of evil, which occasionally manifested itself openly. Many people were demon possessed, and many houses were inhabited by evil spirits.

This was something new and strange to us, and we did

not know how to cope with it. To be truthful, we did not want to. It seemed so very non-Church of England, as well as being scarey. We did not comprehend the power of our Lord, who came to destroy the works of the devil. However, the Lord wanted to use us to set people free, and led us forward.

The first battles came in connection with spiritism. There was a very strong spiritist movement in the area, although the nearest 'church' was five miles away. In particular there was one spiritist lady who held great influence. We prayed for her and about her, but to no apparent effect.

One day I felt an inner urge to tell her that God loved her. This was a shock in more ways than one. If pressed, I would have said of course He loves her, just like He loves all of us. But to tell her. How could I do it? Dare I do it?

The Lord knew my dilemma, and organised things. The next week, when visiting a local hospital, who should I meet in the corridor but the very lady. I realised that this was an intended meeting, and I had to pass on the message there and then. So summoning up all my courage, I stopped in front of her.

'Hello,' I said, 'I have a message from God for you. He loves you.'

I then made a speedy get-away. A week later, at a prayer meeting, a very powerful prayer was offered for her salvation. The next day she was found dead. We were filled with a holy awe. We could see our Father working in this situation. He knew about the spiritist, and the damage she was causing. Yet He loved her, and was using us to seek her soul, even to the end.

Soon after this I was called upon to cast out a demon. The Lord put me in a corner, from which there was no escape. I was visiting a lady who had lapsed from her Christian faith. As we were drinking coffee, I asked her why she had fallen away. She was suddenly convulsed. I knew the convulsion was demonic, and that I had to do something there and then. There was only one Person who could help, so taking the coffee cup out of her hand, and recalling the healing of the epileptic lad, I commanded the evil spirit,

'In the name of Jesus, come out of her.'

Immediately she recovered, picked up her cup of coffee, and carried on talking. She had no idea that anything had happened, but was free from the evil, and soon came back to Christ. My unholy reaction was,

'It works.'

I floated home that evening, knowing something more of the power of the Lord.

This was the start of a ministry which, in time, was shared with a few other members of the church. We saw evil spirits cast out of people, and houses cleansed from resident evil. Truly the Lord is powerful, and keeps His word if we but trust and obey. He is the same God, who promised, and gave, signs and wonders in the Bible days. His power is not diminished, even in these days of faithlessness. His arm is not shortened. If we dare to believe and trust, He will do great things through His church, to the glory of His name and the upbuilding of the body of Christ.

Chapter 8

Commitment

'No one who puts his hand to the plough and looks back is fit for the kingdom of God.' (Luke 9:62)

The train journey between Sheffield and Doncaster cannot claim to be the most scenic in the land. In the nineteen seventies, most of the track was surrounded by steel works, mines and chemical plant. The one point of interest is the keep of Conisborough Castle. This is the best preserved Norman keep in the land. Nowadays most of the industry has disappeared, but the Castle stands replete with a new visitor centre. Perhaps this is a parable of the times.

As I was travelling through this somewhat forbidding part of the land, the Lord spoke to me.

'Peter, if I wish it, will you stay in Blagley all your working life?'

This was a real bombshell.

'What, be committed to stay there **all** my working life? Never to have the luxury of seeking a move when things were going badly? To be a pit village parson for life. Oh, come on, Lord. Surely not?'

I had been at Blagley for about four years, and in the normal run of events I would have been thinking of a move three or four years hence. But now this. I had no doubt that the Lord had spoken to me. It was crystal clear what He was asking of me. He did not say I would stay at Blagley all my life, but that I must be prepared to do so, if He willed. I had to give an open-ended commitment to Him. It took me three weeks to give in.

'Yes, Lord. If you wish it, I will stay all my working life. It is in your hands, not mine,' I finally said, and meant it.

Once the commitment was made, I knew a real freedom. From now on I was committed to the Lord in Blagley. Everything had to be faced. There was no running away. I also had the freedom of knowing that if He wanted me to leave, He would make it clear. There was no need to anxiously scan the Situations Vacant in the Church Times. I could relax, and get on with the job in hand.

Despite first appearances, the Lord was really working for my good. He knew that I was the sort to run away when things got tough, and He wanted to overcome that weakness. Of course, there were times when all this was forgotten, and I wanted to get out of the parish as quickly as possible. But the deep stability of knowing I was working within His will always prevailed.

There is much in Scripture about giving ourselves wholly to our Lord. Jesus emphasises time and again that we are to love Him with all our heart, our soul, our mind and our strength (Mark 12:30). This means a total sacrifice of ourselves, in love, to our Father. Every part of our life must be placed in His hands. Half measures are not enough.

This brings a challenge to those of us who hold to the divine inspiration of the Scripture. We cannot say the Bible is true on an intellectual level only. We must be willing to apply its truth to our whole lives, including our job prospects. No longer can we plan our working life. It must be totally given to Him, and we must be at His disposal, to be used in any way He wants. All thoughts of promotion or advancement must go.

This was just one practical lesson about commitment. There were many more to come. All were based on the wonderful truth that our Lord is wholly committed to us. He gave Himself on the Cross that we might live. Our commitment is therefore our response to His; the difference being that whilst His self-giving is total and perfect, ours is always incomplete and marred by selfishness.

We learned that commitment began at worship. As Christians we had to be willing to come before Him in worship on a regular, disciplined basis. If we were not willing to do that, then we would not be committed to much else. For us, this meant seeking to worship twice every Sunday.

'Sunday is the Lord's Day,' I would natter. 'It is not the Lord's half day, but a full day. We should mark it and sanctify it by coming before Him both morning and evening, so far as we are able.'

This was quite a revolutionary thought to some, and not all accepted it. But many did, and they grew as a result.

We also discovered that commitment does not only apply to matters spiritual.

Brian was a shop-keeper in the village. He owned a furniture store, which was open every day of the week, including Sundays for viewing. He was a good business man, with a nose for a deal. Yet he was a gentle, thoughtful person, who was very approachable.

Brian's wife, Ann, became a Christian. It was a quiet conversion. She simply felt 'someone' telling her to go to church. She made a New Year's Resolution to do so, and came to church on the first Sunday evening of that year. It was not long before she found a deep personal relationship with Jesus.

Ann then started to pray for Brian, and did so for a number of years. Unlike many people in the area, Brian was not against the Church. He was supportive of Ann in her faith, but would go no further.

One summer Ann and Brian had two students staying with them for a month. They were helping in some Christian work in the parish, which was being sponsored by British Youth for Christ. One day Brian saw one of these young men kneeling in prayer in his bedroom, and that brought him to a decision to follow the Lord. He appeared at Church the following Sunday, told me he had come for Jesus, and grew into a beautiful Christian man.

Very soon we noticed a sign on Brian's shop. It said that from now on it was closed every Sunday. Brian had made a stand of real, and potentially costly, commitment to our Lord. Many people asked him why he was doing it.

'It is because I have become a Christian,' he would invariably tell them.

His faithful act of commitment also became a source of Christian witness, and of course, the Lord did not let Brian down.

A further lesson was that commitment to Jesus was even greater than commitment to football matches.

It was June, 1990. England were playing West Germany in the semi-final of the World Cup on a Wednesday evening. The whole country was agog. Everything stopped for the match. Even Parliament was kept informed as it debated the issues of the day.

But we had a problem. Our church youth group always met on a Wednesday evening. What should be done this Wednesday? Should the meeting be cancelled? Or a television brought into the meeting? Frank, the leader, who was a keen sportsman, had to make a decision.

'We meet next Wednesday as normal,' he said, the week before the match. 'God is greater and more important than a football match.'

So the leaders were committed to missing the match that night, or watching a re-run on the video. Maybe there lurked the thought,

'If nobody turns up, we can go home and watch.'

Perhaps a hope that no one would come entered their minds. But they arrived for the meeting, and so did the young members of the group. They met that night as normal; they prayed, they sang, they learned of the Lord, whilst the country was engrossed elsewhere. Surely the Lord was pleased by this simple act of commitment of his faithful people.

Many of us are good at starting a work for the Lord. We are also, sadly, good at dropping it when other things intervene. Yet the Word of God is true, and it tells us that once we have put our hand to the plough, there can be no turning back. If we set out on that road of Christian living and service, then however much the world, the flesh or the devil tries to distract us, we must keep going, and be faithful to our Lord.

One of the saddest stories in the Bible is that of Demas, who deserted Paul, being *'in love with the present world'* (2 Timothy 4:10). Presumably at one time Demas was full of love for Jesus, and desired to serve Him. Yet the love of the world proved the greater. Thus he deserted the Lord's work, and trusted in the world, which is powerless to save.

If we hold that the Bible is true, then we must seek to live by it, and try to be totally committed to Jesus. There can be no escape from this. There is nothing worse than a Christian who claims the Bible is the true, inspired Word of God, and then does not even try to shape his or her life by its precepts. On the other hand true commitment brings great glory to the Lord, and we are thereby blessed and prepared for His coming Kingdom.

Chapter 9

Simple Obedience in Small Things

'He who is faithful in a very little is faithful also in much.'   (Luke 16:10)

Nancy, a retired miner's wife, walked into church one Sunday evening clutching a bunch of flowers. She took her normal seat and put the flowers down beside her. At the end of the service she heard someone crying in the pew behind. It was Kathleen, who usually sat elsewhere in the church, and who for reasons known only to herself and God, had broken down in a flood of tears.

As Kathleen looked up, a bunch of flowers appeared over the top of the pew.

'The Lord told me to take some flowers to church tonight,' said Nancy, 'so they must be for you.'

At the same time as the flowers were offered, the Lord spoke directly to Kathleen. He said,

'You shall not bear this burden alone.'

It was just a small personal incident, noticed by hardly anyone, yet saying so much. The Lord knew how Kathleen was feeling that night, and through an act of simple obedience, she was shown His love and care. Obedience to the Lord, even in the seemingly small things of life, is so important.

There are many occasions in the Bible when people were told to do something which seemed small, and even absurd. Naaman the Syrian was told to wash in the River Jordan. It hurt his pride, but in the end he obeyed and was healed of leprosy. The servants at the wedding at Cana in Galilee were told to fill the jars with water, draw out some and take it to the steward of the feast. They did as they were told, and found the water had turned into wine.

Jesus taught His followers to obey Him implicitly in all things, however small, even when the command seemed to be totally against common sense. Scripture teaches that simple obedience in small things produces great results. This was a lesson we were taught many times at Blagley. In fact, it was such obedience that made for the smooth running of the church, for it was at this level that the Lord dealt lovingly and graciously with our everyday needs and problems.

Lydia taught at an infant's school in a neighbouring parish. She and her husband were active members of the local Baptist church, but they had close links with many members of St Jude's.

One day she had an interview for a post at the infant's school in Blagley. She wanted to be well dressed for the occasion and was troubled because she had no black handbag to match her outfit. As she was contemplating this problem she was told to drive to the interview by a certain road, and she would pick up a handbag on the way. The road was not the most direct route to the school, but, believing this to be of the Lord, she drove the way she was told.

Half way along the journey she saw Rosemary, waiting at a bus stop. Rosemary, a young mother and a member of our congregation at St Jude's was worried. She had been visiting a church member and had missed the bus home. If she was not back home soon her youngest son would arrive from school and find the house empty. She did not know whether to risk waiting for the next bus, or to set off and walk the mile and a half home. She was told,

'Wait at the bus stop and Lydia will pick you up.'

Rosemary knew Lydia would not drive into the village that way, and argued with the Lord, but nonetheless waited at the bus stop. Very soon Lydia appeared and got her home in time. Of course Rosemary was carrying a black hand bag, which Lydia borrowed. The teaching post was offered to Lydia, and she was a great blessing as a Christian teacher in the parish. How wonderfully the Lord cares for all our needs.

Julie, one of our young people, had recently left school and was looking for work. She had been on a work experience scheme with the local Inland Revenue Office, and was very keen to work there. A post had been promised, but no guarantees were given as to when it would be available. Her father owned a shop, and offered her work until she heard from the Tax Office. But Julie did not like the idea of working for father. That seemed worse than no work at all. So she remained unemployed.

After a few weeks a church member was told by the Lord to tell Julie to work for her father, and not be proud. This message was relayed to me, who had the job of telling Julie. Those sort of jobs tended to come to the Vicar.

Julie accepted the word, and told her father she would be willing to work for him after all. But even before she started, a letter arrived from the Inland Revenue, saying she could start at the office in two weeks time. So Julie worked two weeks at her father's shop before moving to the job of her choice.

John and Carrie were an elderly couple. Like many older men in the area, John had respiratory problems, and was also house-bound. I took communion to their home each week, and prayed for his healing, although he did not improve. However, the Lord heard our prayers, and one Sunday morning, in the midst of a Communion service, told Margaret to take a vapour lamp to John and Carrie. This seemed very odd, and somewhat unspiritual to me. I was expecting a mighty and spectacular act of healing. But Margaret did as she was told, and John's problems were largely overcome. The vapour lamp did the trick. Our prayers were answered, but not in the way I had expected. Again, it was a question of simple obedience to instructions from the Lord.

I found it very difficult to accept these simple instructions from the Lord, and had to learn the meaning of the Scripture,

> *'Trust in the Lord with all your heart, and do not rely on your own insight.'* (Proverbs 3:5)

Arrogance of spirit so often prevents the Lord's work moving ahead. We feel we know better than He, and end up by missing opportunities set before us.

Joyce was suffering from schizophrenia. She was happily married, with one child, and a nice house. Yet this terrible shadow was permanently over her life.

She started coming to St Jude's, along with three other friends, and soon settled down into the life of the church. We started to minister to her needs, and felt some progress had been made. Then, quite suddenly, all four stopped coming. This was sad, but it was something we were quite used to. Many people did come, test the waters, and then disappear. I visited Joyce on a number of occasions, and tried to persuade her to return to church, but to no avail. She was not going to come back, and that was that.

About six months later, whilst travelling home from a holiday on the Isle of Wight, Margaret informed me,

'I have to go and see Joyce to bring her back to church.'

'You are wasting your time,' I replied. 'I have tried and failed.'

'No, I have been told to go and see her,' insisted Margaret.

A day or two later, Margaret arranged to visit Joyce. As she approached the street where Joyce lived, she met Joyce standing at the corner, waiting for her. She had been wanting to come back to church, but had not known how to make the first step.

Margaret heard the Lord's instructions, and thankfully ignored my opinions. Joyce returned to the Lord's people. In due course she was miraculously healed of her schizophrenia, and became a great servant of the Lord.

On one occasion I did get it right. David was a member of a church in another part of the town. He was studying for the Non-Stipendiary Ministry of the Church of England, and was to be ordained in two years time. As part of the learning process, he had to spend six months in a parish unlike his home church.

I first heard about him when a fellow-worker of David's from the local hospital, said,

'Do you know David Ottewell?'

'Never heard of him,' I said.

'Well, he feels he has to come to Blagley for six months as part of his training. He'll be getting in touch with you.'

One Sunday David arrived at an Evening Service, with his wife and two friends. We talked after the service, and again a few days later. He said he had prayed about where he should go, and felt the Lord was telling him to come to Blagley.

After praying about it, and consulting with the elders, it seemed right to ask David to come. On this occasion Margaret was not too keen. I was very busy, and she did not like the idea of my taking on another responsibility.

However we accepted him. He arrived in January, 1992,

and at once immersed himself in our church life. In February, I was taken into hospital, and my ministry at Blagley came to a full stop. And there was David, with another five months to go, and no Vicar to lead, guide or teach him anything.

Yet David proved to be the right man in the right place at the right time. As well as helping out in the church in many ways, he was a tower of strength to both Margaret and myself in a time of darkness and near despair. He always appeared when the need was at its greatest, and spoke words of comfort and strength, which helped us through.

The Lord had provided David for both ourselves and the church. David had listened to the Lord, heard the instruction to come to St Jude's, and had obeyed. Through that obedience, the Lord's blessings flowed into a dark situation.

Our Lord promises us in His Word,

> *'I will instruct you and teach you the way you should go; I will counsel you with My eye upon you.'*
>
> (Psalm 32:8)

We are promised that

> *'your ears shall hear a word behind you, saying, "This is the way, walk in it."'*   (Isaiah 30:21)

As we obeyed that still, small voice, we received blessings without number. Through obedience, His work went forward. There is much truth in the hymn by F.W. Faber, which says,

> If our love were but more simple,
> We should take Him at His word;
> And our lives would be all sunshine,
> In the sweetness of our Lord.

Chapter 10

Mammon

'"The silver is mine, and the gold is mine," says the Lord of hosts.' (Haggai 2:8)

Money is the curse and bane of the life of a parish clergyman. The church building has to be kept in repair, and heated, cleaned and insured. None of this can be done without money. The witness of the church in the locality has to be financed. There are many worthy causes which seek financial support from the churches. On top of all this there is the dreaded quota, or parish share, which goes towards paying the Vicar's wages, and the upkeep of the central organisation of the church. The quota is widely resented as a tax upon the parish, with the underlying threat of no quota, no Vicar. The burden of raising the finance usually falls upon the parish priest, and many a ministry has been ruined by the Vicar continually appealing for funds.

One of the truths to which I clung on arriving at Blagley, was that the Lord would provide. The Scriptures teach us that He is the God who provides for His people in every way, materially as well as spiritually. If we trust Him, He does not let us down. We found this to be the case, but as we sought to live by this truth we were led into unexpected situations, and learnt many lessons.

I tried to teach this truth from the very beginning.

'There is no need to raise money for the church,' I would thunder. 'The Lord will provide for all our needs. If we give faithfully, then all will be well. We should not expect people outside the church to support us. What would they think if I went round the parish, cap in hand, asking for donations to the Noble family fund? Neither should we go round asking for donations to the church family fund.'

It was not a message which met with immediate response. After years of money raising, you could not blame church people if they found it hard to grasp that there was a better way. Yet slowly the idea came to be accepted, although not without trials.

Money-raising efforts had to stop. There were not many of them, so that was fairly easy, apart from the raffles.

At my first Church Council meeting I was asked what I thought about raffles. I said I thought they were sinful, that all gambling was sinful, and as God's people we should trust in Him for money. Looking back, I have no doubt that I was overbearing and rather pious, yet right nonetheless.

'But we have a raffle at the Harvest Tea,' they replied.

Problem number one.

'That's alright,' I said. 'You have your raffle, but I will not be there.'

My presence was obviously important that year, as no raffle took place. The Vicar sat back with a smirk, and thought the battle had been won. It had, until the next year, when the raffle was reinstated without the Vicar's knowledge. So what now? How were we to cope with this problem?

After an anxious few days, with much prayer, I preached a sermon denouncing the evils of raffles and of gambling in general, and announced that from now on there was a ban on all gambling on church premises and properties. Then I went home and wondered what would happen next.

To my amazement and delight, most people accepted my leadership in this matter, and raffles were no more. But equally, if not more importantly, the collections went up almost threefold from the next week. Before my sermon the weekly collection was about twelve pounds. On the following Sunday, the collection went up to over thirty pounds, and grew from that level. I could only praise God for His faithfulness, and learn the lesson that if we stick to the truth, He will bless.

Another unexpected result of this stand came a month later. I had written an article for the church magazine about why gambling was wrong. Our local printer was a Christian man, with clear and definite views. He rang me up after reading my script.

'Mr Noble,' he boomed, 'I have just read your article about gambling. I couldn't agree more. I'll print this month's edition free of charge for you.'

What more could we say? Praise the Lord.

There were many more things to learn about giving. The subject of tithing had to be addressed. We worked out that if we trusted the Lord to support us, we must be prepared to give properly. What was the proper way of giving? The answer came very easily – the tithe.

This was another problem. For a start, Margaret and myself had to sort out our own personal giving. If we ourselves did not give according to the biblical precepts, how could I preach and teach about it? Our own house must be put in order first. Only then could I teach the flock.

Teaching about tithing for the first time to a church which has no knowledge of the subject requires the wisdom of Solomon. It would be easy to make it sound as if the Vicar was asking for money yet again. So a time had to be found when we were not particularly short of funds, that is, not in the red. Clear teaching was required to make sure people understood that this was what God said, and not just another of the Vicar's good ideas. We also had to be sensitive not to impose burdens which people could not stand. Many people who joined us were up to the hilt in debt, and quite unable to manage their money. If I had been heavy about tithing they could have been given the impression that unless they tithed then and there they had no real place in the church. They had to be shown that tithing was right, but in some cases it had to be approached in the context of clearing debts and learning to manage personal income.

The teaching was given, with trembling knees and a heart near the mouth. Again, I was amazed how people accepted the truth. The Holy Spirit was clearly at work in hearts and minds, and so long as a teaching could be shown to be scriptural it was accepted.

Obviously many people did have difficulty with tithing. An immediate reaction was,

'I cannot afford it.'

We learned, as time went on, to encourage by saying,

'You cannot afford **not** to tithe.'

Here the promise of Malachi 3:10 became real to us,

> *'Bring the full tithe into the storehouse ... and thereby put me to the test, says the Lord of hosts, if I will not open the windows of heaven for you and pour down for you an overflowing blessing.'*

Malcolm was in his early twenties. He was an unemployed member of the church, and new in the faith. He claimed he could not afford to tithe, because he was on unemployment benefit. However, it was not long before he was convicted that he should tithe, even on the dole. One week he took the plunge and put ten per cent of his dole money into the church collection. Before the week was out he received an unexpected cheque for over two hundred pounds from the dole office. They had been underpaying him, and had just discovered their error.

A coincidence? No. The Lord was showing the truth of His Word, and honouring someone who had struggled and finally obeyed.

As the Lord provided for our needs, a number of other blessings came our way. One result was that the church treasurer was brought to a deeper faith as he saw the money coming in, despite no fund raising. Another was that the church was set free to do the things that mattered. No longer was it bound by raising money. We had time to minister and share our Lord with each other and with the world. We could approach the world with something to give, rather than with a begging bowl. Leaders of the children's work were set free to teach the children. We had confidence in the Lord that the church would provide for all their financial needs. Sunday School teachers, for example, no longer had to raise money for the Sunday School. It was their job to teach, not to be money raisers.

Along with the blessings came hard lessons. We were taught, for example, that the Lord expected all bills to be paid, including the quota. At one time we were going through an anti-establishment patch, and not bothering about whether we paid the quota. We adopted the attitude that we would pay if we had the money, but we would not make it a top priority. The net result was, that at the start of one year in the late nineteen eighties we were owing twelve thousand pounds in quota. This was more than our total yearly income. But in our self-satisfied manner we did not bother. However, the Lord did.

Around the February of that year, a church member who had a gift of prophecy, came to me and said,

'Peter, the Lord says we must give to Caesar what belongs to Caesar.'

My heart sank, for I knew it meant we must pay the

quota. However, I contrived to forget it. After all she might have been wrong, and all prophecy must be tested.

Three weeks later another church member came, and said,

'Peter, I don't know what this means, but we must give to Caesar what belongs to Caesar.'

This time all opposition collapsed. There had been no collusion between the two members, yet both came with the same message. So after the usual fearful week I shared this word with the church, and said we must pay this money as best we could. I had no idea where the money would come from. I doubted if we could find half of it. Things were economically bad after the nineteen eighty-four miner's strike, and the closure of the smokeless fuel plant two years later had done nothing to help. However some money did come in and we reached just over two thousand pounds. This was sent to the diocese, and we thanked the Lord for what we had received. But what about the other ten thousand?

One morning three months later the church treasurer rang me up, almost incoherent with joy.

'This is a great day for the church. What a wonderful thing. It's a miracle.'

'Hold your horses; what's the matter?' said I.

'There is over ten thousand pounds in the collection this week, earmarked to pay the quota,' came the reply.

After recovering we praised the Lord and paid the quota. God knew it could be done, and He moved the hearts of people to give. If only we trusted Him more simply.

Despite providing for us financially, the Lord never let us become rich. Our bank balance was normally just in the black, and no more. In a similar vein, we often had to wait until the last minute before enough money came in to pay the bills. This taught us to pray continually for the finance we needed, and wait in trust. It also helped us not to take the Lord for granted. Sadly there were times when complacency crept in, and our giving went down, but He loved us enough to shake us out of it.

We also had to learn that there were times when the Lord would say no to our requests for finance.

In nineteen eighty three we moved to a new Vicarage. The original Vicarage was too big for us, so a smaller house was built at the bottom of the garden. The diocese put the old Vicarage up for sale, and the majority of the church (including the Vicar) thought we should seek to buy it as a parish centre. We had been without a church hall for a number of years, and premises were needed. At least, that was our idea. We were quite carried away with the plan, although some brave souls were not in favour.

On this occasion the majority got it wrong. It was not in the Lord's will for us to buy the property and the money did not come in, even though we asked Him to provide. In the end the coal strike overtook us, with a consequent lack of money, and the property was sold to a private buyer. Later we saw that we were wrong, and praised God that He protected us from the folly of our own enthusiasm.

In all these ways we found that He is the Lord who provides. He is as good as His Word. May His name be praised.

Chapter 11

Ministry

'And His gifts were that some should be apostles, some prophets, some evangelists, some pastors and teachers, to equip the saints for the work of ministry, for building up the body of Christ.' (Ephesians 4:11)

'Stop the parish, I want to get off!'

Many clergy work under great pressure. They face demands from both the diocese, and the parish. Those from the diocese normally come by post, but those from the parish are on the doorstep. Should a church grow in numbers, grass root demands increase, with more people on the Vicarage doorstep.

Most ministers genuinely try to meet all demands, taking it upon themselves to cope with everything that comes their way. They feel this is part of their calling, and they must do the best they can. The results, however, soon show in their personal and in their ministerial lives. They become ratty and irritable. They may work harder, which inevitably means less time for their own spiritual life, and for the family. Alternatively, they may withdraw into themselves, doing less and less work. They might pray for the wings of the dove, so that they can fly away and be at peace. 'Lord, get me out of here,' is a common clergy prayer. Sadly, they might stop praying altogether, and justify it by the great work load. When all else fails, a letter is sent to the bishop, using such phrases as,

'I feel I have fulfilled my ministry in this place,'

'I believe the Lord is calling me forward,' or

'I think it would be better for the parish if they had a change of leader.'

It is possible to use all sorts of right-sounding phrases, and yet all the time there is a bleeding heart, and a sense of failure at being unable to get a grasp of the job.

Church members notice when the Vicar is going under, and react in different ways. Some grumble, 'He's not what he used to be. He's getting past it.' Others are sympathetic, and will suggest the need of extra help. The genuinely sympathetic will offer themselves, and try to take some of the load.

There were many times in my ministry at Blagley when I felt I had reached the end of my tether. On one such occasion, I read the bishop's exhortation in the Prayer Book Ordination service. I thought I had better get back to basics and see what I was supposed to do. It turned out to be an act of self-immolation, which only increased my sense of inadequacy and failure. For I was exhorted to be a messenger, watchman and steward of the Lord. I had to teach, premonish (whatever that might mean), feed and provide for the Lord's family. I was to seek for Christ's sheep that are dispersed abroad. I had to be studious in reading and learning the Scriptures, to pray continually, and to be a wholesome and godly example to the flock committed to my care. Just to drive it home, I was reminded that should the church, or any member thereof, take hurt or hindrance by reason of my neglect, then I had to know the greatness of my fault, and also the horrible punishment that would ensue.

'Lord,' I prayed, 'how can one man possibly do all this?'

At such times I learned to turn to the Bible for answers, and I was not disappointed. Slowly but surely, my eyes were opened, and I was shown many wonderful truths about God's organisation of His church.

Perhaps the most important discovery was that God does not expect one man to carry the whole burden of ministry. In the early days of the Exodus from Egypt, Moses tried to take all the leadership upon himself. He judged the people from morning till evening. His father-in-law, Jethro, saw what was going on, and rebuked Moses.

> *'What you are doing is not good. You and the people with you will wear yourselves out, for the thing is too heavy for you; you are not able to perform it alone.'*
>
> (Exodus 18:17, 18)

He told Moses to appoint able and trustworthy men to judge the people, so that he need only deal with the hard cases. The work of caring for God's people had to be shared. Every Vicar should have his personal Jethro.

Our eyes were also opened to the ministry of elders and deacons. In the beginning of the Christian era, each local church had a group of elders or presbyters, who derived their authority from the Apostles. Their task was to care for the church, and build it up into Christ. This was a team effort, not a one man show, although it appears from Revelation that there was a leading elder, known as the angel.

The elders were local church members, who were set aside for their task by the Apostles or their delegates. Leaders were not imported from outside.

Alongside the elders were the deacons, who dealt with the temporal matters of church life. The first deacons, for example, saw to the feeding of the widows, leaving the Apostles free to pray and preach (Acts 6:1–6). It was comforting to read that the Apostles were led to appoint deacons due to the pressure of their work.

If the Bible is true in all it says, the organisation of the early church must be equally right for the church in our generation. This took some time to register, as our traditional Anglican background was very different. However, we gritted our teeth, and tried to adapt our local church structure to conform with the biblical pattern.

This was a slow and halting journey of faith, with many mistakes along the way. We had to carry the whole church along with us, and we could only advance one step at a time, testing the waters as we went. It was also an unfinished journey. For example, although we appointed elders, we never sorted out the position and role of deacons.

We were also led to consider eldership through another route, that of anointing the sick with oil. Since we are told in James 5, that the sick should call for the elders (in the plural) of the church, the inevitable question arose – who are the elders? This was not the flashpoint which led us into setting up an eldership, but it reinforced our will to do so.

As we began to grasp the nettle of appointing elders, we had to face a number of questions. Who should be elders? How should they be appointed? What qualifications were required?

As we looked to the Bible, in particular the Pastoral Epistles, we saw that an elder must be the husband of one wife. Leaving aside the question of whether elders can be single as well as married, they should certainly be men, and not bigamists. We had men in the church, and none of them were bigamists, so we were in business. We saw other qualifications which are fearful. Elders are to be blameless, upright, holy, self-controlled, in fact men of high moral standing and Christian maturity. Again, we had such men.

We also realised that the local church did not elect elders. It was not like voting for a Parochial Church Council. In the early church the Apostles decided who should be elders. As we had no Apostle to turn to, we had to do the best we could. Hence I made it clear that, as Vicar, the choice of elder was mine, but I was happy to receive any prayerful thoughts from church members about who should be appointed. This required a great deal of spiritual maturity amongst church members. It also meant, especially amongst the men, a willingness to accept those chosen, without feelings of personal bitterness or rancour.

At first, three men were chosen, whom we described as Pastoral Elders. Their tasks were to administer the chalice at Communion, anoint the sick with oil, and to help in the general pastoral care of the church. This worked very well and was a means of great blessing. I was delighted that the church accepted this way of working, and members were not upset when an elder visited instead of the Vicar. In fact, most were delighted. As time went by, we found people approaching an elder with a problem, instead of going to the Vicar. Later we were driven to appoint more elders, as the work was becoming too much for the original three. Our final arrangement was six elders, plus Vicar.

Most of the elders were well-upholstered gentlemen, and an extra-biblical qualification that only men with a certain girth could be elders, was suggested by various church members. After this, we were never quite sure whether other men in the church fasted in the hope of avoiding being appointed, or over-indulged with the opposite aim in mind. Such was the joy and sense of fun we had within the church.

We quickly discovered that there were different gifts within the eldership. Ben, for example, was a pastor, who had a gift of caring, especially for older folk. He also had a gift of casting out evil spirits. Frank had a gift of working with young people, and of evangelism. Brian was a man who could go deeply into prayer, and would be able to tell us some direct things from the Lord. Dave and Frank were able preachers and teachers. As well as being excellent in practical tasks, Laurie seemed to bring with him a sense of peace whenever he visited the sick. Ian soon showed he had a God-given capacity for leadership, and a way of holding people together in the Lord.

The weekly elder's meeting became a good time for sharing burdens and problems. Many clergy have to go outside the parish to find fellowship and support. This was not the case for myself. All the support I needed was normally found within the church.

Problems naturally arose as we sought to move to this scriptural system of ministry. We had to think about the relationship between the Parochial Church Council and the Eldership. Tensions were experienced here, as it was felt by some that the elders were doing the work of the Council. Another problem was that of gifted individuals within the church. How should people with prophetic gifts be recognised, accepted and used? How can those with gifts of healing be integrated into the healing work of the church? How does their ministry key in with a working eldership?

Many of these, and similar, problems were not fully resolved during our time at Blagley. But nevertheless, we went far enough along the scriptural path of ministry to know that here was God's answer to all the pressures of ministry which are found in the church. He lays down His way of working, and if we trust and follow, then He will build His church. His Word can be relied upon, at all times and in all circumstances.

Chapter 12

And the Greatest of These

'A new commandment I give to you, that you love one another; even as I have loved you, that you also love one another. By this all men will know that you are my disciples, if you have love for one another.'

(John 13:34, 35)

Trafalgar Square, New Year's Eve, 1983. The old year had a quarter of an hour to run.

The crowd was happy, people were singing, and girls were kissing the policemen. We were spending a few days in London to recuperate from the Christmas marathon which every Vicar has to face.

The clock struck midnight. The crowd went crazy. I wondered what the New Year would bring. The very year, 1984, seemed to be loaded with significance. Would it be much the same as usual, or would there be some Orwellian twist to it all?

In March word went round the village, 'The pit's out.' The great coal strike of 1984 had begun. The men at the threatened Cortonwood Colliery went on strike in a vain endeavour to protect their jobs. Very soon the whole of the British coalfield, apart from Nottinghamshire, had joined them.

We had no idea how long the strike would last, or what

the results would be, but we were aware of many potential conflicts within the church. The congregation, which had been growing steadily, included a number of miners, who were all on strike. We also had some pit deputies, who were not on strike. Added to that, there were those who worked at the Coalite smokeless fuel plant, the local power stations and in the mining supply industry. Perhaps all of these would be on short time or laid off because of the strike. Some people in the church supported the strike; others regarded it with horror. It only needed one word in the wrong place to cause untold trouble, and that was not a hard thing to accomplish amongst our band of pilgrims. Here was a real test for us.

On the first Sunday of the strike I tried to make sure we all knew the score. I stressed that whatever our personal views, we were first and foremost Christians, and therefore we should always, at all times, love one another as our Lord Jesus commands. This love should be shown in our willingness to accept one another, and to support and care for each other. We must show that Christian love transcends everything. This was our line all through the year-long strike. We did not take sides as a church. but tried to show God's love to all.

It was not an easy option. Quite apart from the feelings of our individual church members, we were very much aware that leading church authorities supported one side only. Letters to the press, and public statements, told us that we should be partisan, and make a social or political point. This was not lost on some of the more radical union members in the area, who told us that our bosses supported them and so should we.

But the proof of the pudding was in the eating. We experienced a great overflowing of love within the church. We did not grow in numbers, but we grew together in love in a completely new way. There were hairy moments when it looked as if people would crack. Many of them were, after all, under great pressure; yet the love which the Spirit brings held us together, to the glory of God.

The immediate result of the strike, so far as our community was concerned, was lack of money. The Union did not give strike pay, and there was no state benefit for the men. An allowance was available for wives and children, but it was hardly enough to keep body and soul together. Married couples were drawing just over six pounds per week, and couples with two children were getting around twenty five pounds per week.

As well as having a devastating effect on household budgets and bringing great strains into some marriages, the lack of money led to a huge reduction in church collections. Our income went down by fifty per cent after the first week of the strike, and we ended up with about thirty pounds per week. It would not even pay the quota. Yet many of our mining families still continued to tithe. However much came in, the first tenth belonged to the Lord. It was a wonderful example of Christian giving and commitment.

Very soon a sharing network grew up between church members. Those who had money gave to those who had none. Five pound notes passed from Christian to Christian. I was given many an envelope with the instructions to give this to so-and-so. It all happened spontaneously, with no hectoring from the pulpit. The Holy Spirit was moving the hearts of Christians to love one another, not just in word but also in deed.

In many ways the situation was like that of the early church as recorded in Acts chapter 4, verse 32, where

> '*the company of those who believed were of one heart and soul, and no one said that any of the things which he possessed was his own, but they had everything in common.*'

Although most of us were poor at that time, yet in His way, the Spirit organised things so that we were enabled to share what we had, and support each other.

The story of Jean's fifty pence gives the flavour of the times. It was the season of Lent. Jean's husband, Russ, was on strike, but they continued to tithe. One Sunday Jean had fifty pence in her purse. It was her last piece of money, and she had promised it to the Lord as her Lenten offering, over and above the tithe. Whilst in church, the obvious temptation came along.

'Do not give it. It will be of more use to you. It will help to feed the children.'

Yet she overcame the tempter, and gave her coin to the Lord.

As she walked down the church path after the service, someone put a five pound note into her hand. By the time she reached the church gate she had been given another fiver. Giving her fifty pence to the Lord had resulted in the overflowing blessing of ten pounds.

But there is a twist to the tale. In the street outside the church, Jean saw Dawn, whose husband, Frank, was also on strike. So Jean took the first five pound note home, and Dawn took the other.

Sylvia's husband, Colin, worked at the Smokeless Fuel plant. He was on very short time because the coal stock had almost run out. However, they were in receipt of state benefits. Across the road lived Betty and her husband, Jim, who was on strike. Realising their situation, Sylvia took a parcel of food to Betty, because she could not see a fellow-Christian suffering. From a worldly point of view, Sylvia could have been bitter towards Jim. He was partially responsible for Colin being laid off. But as a Christian such feelings could not be given house room, and love prevailed.

Political and social viewpoints did not come into the reckoning. If a fellow Christian was in trouble, he had to be helped. I recall one afternoon riding in the car of a member of the church, delivering some food parcels to families of those on strike. My driver was a staunch Conservative (yes, we did have some, even in a pit village), who told me in no uncertain terms what he would do to the leader of the miner's union. It was a good job the police did not hear us, otherwise he might have been had up for incitement to violence, if not murder. Yet, at the same time, he was helping those on strike. Whatever his political opinions, because he was a Christian he had to help his fellow believers. That came first. That was true love.

Money and food were not the only things that were shared. So was hot water. Part of the miner's wage was free coal. This stopped during the strike. All miner's homes had open fires and fire-back boilers, so there was soon no hot water for the strikers. Unless the washing machine heated the water, the clothes could not be washed, and hot baths became a thing of the past. It was not long before church members who had other means of water heating were washing striker's clothes, and many a striker's family was seen going to another Christian's house for a bath. Again this happened spontaneously. As people realised the need, so they responded. All this was of the Spirit. Although we lacked material goods, we were spiritually rich. He was in charge, and His people were responding.

As the strike wore on into the summer and then the autumn, other churches became aware of our plight. Some were local, whilst others were in the then more affluent south. Food parcels arrived, along with sacks of potatoes, and toys at Christmas. A Christian charity in Switzerland even gave a free holiday to sixty children from our church and area. Yet we never asked for help, or shouted about our problems. We sought to love one another, and the Holy Spirit arranged things. He knew the need, and provided the willing hearts to respond.

Just before Christmas, 1984, our choirmaster, Ian, and his wife, Dorothy, held the usual party for choir members at their home. It was a sign of their care and compassion that many non-choir people were invited that year. About ten o'clock, as the party was at its height, there was a loud knock on the door. A late party-goer? The police? Neither. On the step stood a member from a house church in Doncaster, with thirty frozen chickens for those in need.

It was the best party stopper ever. The fowls had to be delivered there and then. We quickly made a list of church members on strike. Then we added more names until thirty families had been put together. The few people with cars rushed around the village, delivering chickens, often knocking people out of bed. One party-goer was Johnnie, who was on strike. He volunteered to use his car for delivery, but he was almost out of petrol. Never mind. The Lord would provide. And He did. Johnnie rushed here and there with the melting birds, and never ran out of fuel. At one house he knocked up a fellow miner, and gave him a chicken. The recipient was so overwhelmed that he took Johnnie in his arms and kissed him. It was a story Johnnie told us later, with a mixture of laughter and embarrassment.

Despite the lack of money, many people said that Christmas, 1984, was the best Christmas they had ever known. There was a special outpouring of love and joy at that time, despite the worsening situation.

The church was packed for our annual carol service, with many being unable to get into the building. People in the area were seeking something better, and their minds were turning back to God. We learned anew that the core of the season was the birth of our Saviour, and not all the commercialism with which the world has overlaid this festival.

The strike brought many problems in its wake. Great tensions arose within families, and many had to face hard decisions. A lot of the younger miners had started to buy their own homes, and were unable to pay their mortgages. Even the most sympathetic building society could not alleviate the pressures that were on these young married couples. There was also the problem of the man of the house having nothing to do all day. Sadly, many marriages broke down under these strains. No marriages within the church gave way, but much work was required in helping families in difficulties. A number of church members found themselves being used in this area, both within the church and in the wider community.

An increasing problem was an upsurge of illness. Many wives and mothers did without food, so that they could feed their husbands and children. As the autumn and winter drew on, people were cold as their coal ran out. Hence more sickness followed. We had our share of such illness in the church, and here again much time was spent in care and support.

The miners in the church had to face some difficult decisions. Was it right for a Christian to picket? What would happen if violence erupted, as it frequently did? These questions had to be faced. They were big issues at the time, and once more we needed to be close to each other in love, understanding each person's point of view, and the pressures they were under.

One of the highlights of the latter days of the strike was a Service of Reconciliation one Sunday evening in November. The impetus for this came from one of our Church Wardens, Reg, a godly man, who was a pit deputy. The whole village was going through a period of great tension. There had been considerable violence in the streets round the pit, and many people were shell-shocked. The fabric of our area seemed to be collapsing by the day. Hence there was great need for an act of reconciliation before God. We invited representatives from all the unions at the mine, and from the other industries of the area; along with management, local councillors and members of the local police force. The service was also advertised throughout the parish.

We realised that humanly speaking we were taking a big risk. No one might respond. The ill-feeling which was rife in the area might show itself at the service. Nevertheless we found that most of those invited turned up, including our two, much maligned, local bobbies, wearing their police uniform.

Towards the end of the service we invited members of the congregation to share a handshake of peace, as a sign that we were willing to try to live at peace with one another. A most amazing thing happened. Many members of the congregation, some whom I knew were very anti-police, went across to the two policemen and shook them by the hand. The whole congregation was filled with emotion, and many were in tears. The Spirit was again at work, breaking down barriers in the love of God.

The strike was clearly collapsing as it approached its first anniversary. Nobody dared to say so in so many words, but in our hearts we all knew how it would end. This brought in a great fear for the future. Things were never going to be the same again. Urgent and ugly questions arose. Would the pit be closed for good? What were the prospects for future work? Were young men doomed to spend a life-time on the dole? Would anybody care? In this time of despair, there was an even greater need to encourage and uphold each other. None of us knew what the future held, but we could stand together, cry together, laugh together, and trust in our God who never lets us down.

Everything about the strike, and its aftermath, schooled us in the knowledge of God's love. We learned to love each other, just as we were. We learned, in a new way, to be aware of each other's needs, and translate that awareness into loving action. All this was of the Spirit, who filled us and led us in the ways of love. The glory of that year belonged solely to our great and loving God.

Jesus told us that if we love one another, the world will know that we are His disciples. The ancient world looked at Christians with great amazement.

'Behold,' they said, 'how these Christians love one another.'

The reality of local Christians loving each other in this way is a most powerful witness to our Lord. Although we did not grow in numbers during the strike, we experienced a large growth in church membership some six months later, under the stimulus of the Billy Graham Mission in Sheffield. I have no doubt that the love we showed in the strike made this possible. Love is indeed the greatest of these.

Epilogue

'If you continue in my word, you are truly my disciples, and you will know the truth, and the truth will make you free.' (John 8:31, 32)

The aim of this book has been to stress the truth of the Bible, and to show that this truth can be verified by simple obedience. God is not a liar. His Word can be trusted as a basis for Christian living. It was this realisation that motivated our lives and upon which we sought to build up the life of the Body of Christ in Blagley.

Christians who base their lives on the truth of God's Word grow and develop in Him. They are not exempt from times of pain, doubt and uncertainty, but as they are sustained and fed by the Scriptures they emerge triumphant. On the other hand those who trim His Word, using their own judgement to choose what they will accept, always decrease in spiritual stature. They shrivel up in their faith and in due course dry up altogether. The life of Christ, which was in them, slowly dies away and they are left with an emptiness and a deep sadness at what might have been.

With great regret I recall many people who took the latter path. After an initial joy and springtime in the presence of Jesus, they fell away through lack of trust, and became shells of their former selves. Yet I praise God for many who have been faithful to Him and trusted His Word. They tried to follow, even when all around were telling them to deny Him. They struggled to do right, when it would have been easier to do wrong. And the result is plain to see. They have grown into mature Christians, abounding in the works of the Lord.

The same observation is true for churches. If a church seeks to live by the Word of God then it will grow. Yes, it will go through bad patches. It will face times of temptation and decline, and it will have to face great onslaughts from the enemy. But if it remains in the truth of God's Word it will ripen and mature, becoming a beautiful witness for Jesus.

Denial of the truth of the Bible has dire consequences, not only for faith, but also for morality. By ditching the truth, people become enslaved by ways which the Bible says are sinful. Wrong belief always goes hand in hand with wrong behaviour. This can be seen in the Scripture. The false teachers of 2 Peter, chapter 2, for example, who *'secretly bring in destructive heresies,'* are licentious and greedy people, who *'have eyes full of adultery'* (verses 1–3, 14). Similarly, the false teachers mentioned in 2 Timothy, chapter 3, who *'oppose the truth'* (verse 8) are also *'lovers of self, lovers of money, proud, arrogant, abusive, disobedient to their parents'* (verse 2). It is not surprising that those who peddle heretical views, also uphold sub-Christian standards of living.

If we do not hold firmly to the truth of the Scriptures, we will end up in moral as well as spiritual anarchy. And who can deny that we are seeing such anarchy all around us both in church and nation?

At Blagley we saw in a small way that God does honour us when we dare to trust His Word. Had we been more obedient we would have seen more of His power and love.

Moses was far more trusting. In Exodus 39 and 40 we read of the construction of the Tabernacle in the wilderness. We are told that *'as the Lord had commanded; so they had done it'* (Exodus 39:43), and when the work was completed *'the glory of the Lord filled the Tabernacle'* (Exodus 40:34).

If we have faith to trust the Scriptures, we will find that God will work through us in far more amazing and wonderful ways than we can ask or think. His glory will indeed fill our lives, our churches and our land.

To Him be glory for ever and ever. Amen.